THE SUPER
COUPON SHOPPING
SYSTEM

Also by Susan Samtur

Cashing In at the Checkout

THE *Super Coupon Shopping System*

Ingenious New Ways to Save
$$$$ on Every Shopping Bill

SUSAN SAMTUR

A STONESONG PRESS BOOK

NEW YORK

Design and type: Foster Graphic

Illustrations: Perry R. Barrell

The product and brand names mentioned in this book are registered trademarks of the companies that own them.

All coupon use must comply with manufacturers' individual restrictions and regulations.

Library of Congress Cataloging-in-Publication Data

    Samtur, Susan J.

    The Super Coupon Shopping System : ingenious new ways to save $$$$ on every shopping bill / by Susan Samtur.

       p.   cm.

    ISBN 1-56282-797-9

    1. Shopping—United States. 2. Coupons (Retail trade)—United States. 3. Discount—United States. 4. Rebates—United States.

    I. Title.

    TX335.S19 1994

    380. 1'45'0002573—dc20   93-5612

                                                CIP

First Edition

10 9 8 7 6 5 4 3 2 1

Contents

ACKNOWLEDGMENTS   vii

INTRODUCTION   viii

STEP ONE   **Understanding the Retail Structure**   1

What Shoppers Want / Manufacturers: The Cult of Progress / Manufacturers: Retailers' Limits / Consumers: Manufacturers' Allies? / Manufacturers' Tools I: Realistic Imagining / Manufacturers' Tools II: Satisfaction / Manufacturers' Tools III: Money for You / Supermarkets: The Power in the Middle / Step-One Summary

STEP TWO   **Coupons: Shopping for (Almost) Free**   25

Their Number and Objectives / Where to Find Coupons / Keeping Coupons Under Control / Planning the Shopping Trip: Combine, Combine, Combine / Planning the Shopping Trip: The List / In the Store / Step-Two Summary

STEP THREE   **Refunding: Money from Shopping**   51

Refunding Explained / The Process / Falling Through the Cracks / Three Easy Steps: The Refunder's SOS / Saving / Organize Everything / Send, Send, Send / Keeping Records / Step-Three Summary

STEP FOUR   **Shoppers' Networks**   89

Our Own Newsletters / Meeting Other Refunders / Sharing the Wealth: Four Types of Trades / *Refundle Bundle*: A Newsletter's Contents / Step-Four Summary

STEP FIVE   **Gifts Every Day**   103

Types of Free Gifts / Four-Way Savings / Who's
Embarrassed? / Cash-Plus Deals / Points Clubs /
Trading Stamps / Step-Five Summary

STEP SIX   **The Select Coupon Program**   113

Coupons by Choice, Not Chance / Select Coupon
Program / The Official Coupon Supplier / Preferred
Coupon Supplier / High-Demand Coupons /
Step-Six Summary

APPENDIX A: **The Refunder's Glossary**   124

APPENDIX B: **National Brands to Save**   127

APPENDIX C: **Selected Manufacturers' Addresses**   130

APPENDIX D: **UPCs of Selected Products**   140

APPENDIX E: **State Abbreviations**   144

APPENDIX F: **Clearinghouse Addresses**   145

              Refunder's Log   146

*I wish to thank Ken Packman for his significant
writing and editorial work on this book.
I could not have written it without him.*

*I'd also like to thank three others
who contributed extensively:
Carla Byrnes for a first-rate editing job,
Sheree Bykofsky for her super editorial
and production direction,
and Paul Fargis who made this book happen.*

Introduction

--- ✂

26,430 OPPORTUNITIES. The typical modern supermarket displays 26,430 diverse items on its shelves. And every one of those items is an opportunity to make money—not just for grocers, shippers, and manufacturers, but also for those struggling at the end of the retail food chain: consumers.

Unbelievable as it may seem, the vehicles for these chances at consumer prosperity are provided by grocers and manufacturers, whose competition with each other leads to our remarkable benefits. The vehicles? Those seemingly trivial scraps of paper: coupons and rebate offers.

Twenty years ago when I began collecting and using these "scraps," my principal motivation was pretty simple: I wanted, in fact *needed*, to save money. But I was also influenced by another trend of my generation: the desire to make all aspects of my life, including the most mundane, fun. I have been enormously successful in accomplishing both goals.

My success, of course, is due to the System. Twenty years ago my friend Jenny introduced me to her "refund book." My initial scoffing at this bargain nut's latest scheme turned into the sincerest form of admiration as I shamelessly copied, and then enhanced, the concepts I found in that little notebook.

The Super Coupon Shopping System is the result of

Jenny's book and of years spent refining her ideas. It is a simple approach to organizing the multitude of bargains offered by manufacturers and merchants into an opportunistic program of extensive consumer savings.

The most public, and thrilling, demonstrations of the System's success have come on television. One Thursday morning in 1978, Betty Furness and camera crews from the *Today* show accompanied me on a shopping expedition. The show's viewers, then coping with the double economic whammy of stagnation and inflation, were treated to the rare sight of a shopper, me, greeting the tally of my purchases with a huge smile and a fistful of colored pieces of paper that paid 95 percent of that cash register total. I left that supermarket pushing two shopping carts containing groceries costing $130.18, for which I had paid $7.07.

In the fifteen years since that first televised super-shopping trip, I have performed the same magic about two hundred times for shows broadcast throughout the United States. I've appeared in Chicago, Cleveland, Philadelphia, Oklahoma City, Dallas, Atlanta, and Los Angeles with such hosts as Oprah, Donahue, Merv, Richard Simmons, and Regis and Kathie Lee. It's been fun, and it's been profitable.

I don't make these trips with any special help or even encouragement from stores or manufacturers. The only help I use is the help that is available to everyone, and I mean, of course, coupons. I also do not spend extraordinary amounts of time on these trips or on the system that makes them possible, as my last appearance on *Live with Regis and Kathie Lee*, in January 1990, nicely illustrated.

I arrived at the studios at 9:00 A.M., clutching my

rather worn envelope of coupons. I was presented with the advertising flyer of a Food Emporium supermarket near the studio. Five minutes later, I was on the air, discussing with Regis and Kathie Lee my system and planning an immediate shopping trip to the store. At 9:12 I left the studio to begin that shopping trip.

Just twenty-nine minutes later, the hosts of the show, which is broadcast live, joined me at the Food Emporium checkout counter, where the last of my purchases were being rung up. In those twenty-nine minutes I had assembled groceries costing $144.19. Well, in this day of exorbitant prices, that wasn't very difficult. The difficulty arose in the next step of the checkout process; I had with me only the ten dollars given me by Regis, a very tattered envelope, and an audience of New York City shoppers attracted by the television cameras. I took from that tattered envelope a sheaf of coupons and handed them to the checker. She began passing each over the scanner, occasionally clarifying purchases with me. Each pass decreased the total on the cash register display. With the last pass, a coupon for a free bottle of liquid Cheer, the total changed from $2.12 to –$1.87. The store owed *me* money.

I returned the ten dollars to Regis, explaining that I was going to receive ten dollars anyway through a rebate finalized by the Cheer purchase, gave a very pregnant Kathie Lee a package of Luvs Deluxe disposable diapers, and wheeled my free groceries out to my car. That's $144 of merchandise I gained in less than a half an hour. I think that's a better pay scale than even most lawyers get these days.

Granted, I don't always do that well. Ginny, a checker at my local supermarket, estimates that I save 70 percent at least on my regular shopping trips. Ginny also told me, after the first time she rang up one of my super-shopping trips, "You're some buyer. That's the only way to buy." I have to admit that reactions like that, from checkers and from other customers, give me almost as much satisfaction as does the actual financial savings I enjoy.

Another benefit I receive is membership in a national community of couponers and refunders. Over the years I've appeared at hundreds of malls across the country, speaking about the Super Coupon Shopping System. Everywhere, in the South, Midwest, and the West, people welcome and accept me, even overlooking my very definite New York accent. The basis of their acceptance is the common culture we share.

It is a culture bonded by similar stories and language. The stories and language are not just about how individuals save money but about how we all help each other save. There's great joy, and some boasting, in sharing with others methods used to gain greater discounts or to ferret out special refund offers. Our culture is based upon our shared needs to make shopping profitable and upon the network we've created to share the information that results in our rewards.

The profits are great. Over the last twenty years, the System, through organized and opportunistic use of coupons alone, has cut my grocery bills at least in half. I also get paid, directly from manufacturers, between $1,200 and $1,800 every year in cash refunds.

This refund money has made a substantial difference in our lives. One year, when we were struggling to maintain our mortgage payments, it gave us the necessary breathing space by paying all our heating costs. Another year, when things were improved, it provided us with a respite from the New York winter by financing a Florida vacation. During the last ten years, the money has been deposited into a bank account earmarked for our children's college funding. With compounded interest, that account, with its principal derived only from refunds, has grown to over $35,000. All from little scraps of paper and cardboard.

So what is this Super Coupon Shopping System? To begin with, it's something with which most Americans already have some familiarity. At its base is the simple coupon. Most of us have been unable to resist using the occasional coupon offering savings of $1 on a can of coffee or 75 cents on a box of detergent. In fact, industry surveys show that over 75 percent of all multiperson households regularly redeem at least one coupon a week. And most households with children are also already novice refunders, clipping from cereal boxes offers for free baseballs, cassette tapes, stop watches, and "mystery surprises."

But most Americans are not doing this in a systematic manner. There is obviously a world of difference between saving a dollar on a can of coffee and cutting your entire grocery bill in half, or between receiving an occasional "mystery surprise" and making a serious dent in the cost of your children's college education. The difference is the System. And these days, with steady employment as dubious as increased costs for everything are assured, financial security is no longer reliably available through established institutions. The principles that follow establish the six steps of the Super Coupon Shopping System and help provide a measure of that security.

• **Step One** of the Super Coupon Shopping System is to understand the grocery retailing structure. We'll examine the methods used by retailers and manufacturers to shake loose every possible dollar from consumers. Here I'll also discuss how retailers and manufacturers engage in their own hard-fought competitions to lure every possible consumer away from their competitors. But in the end, savvy consumers can use this competition to their advantage.

We'll see how the information age has given supermarkets tools of ever-increasing sophistication in their attempts to target specific consumers, manage merchandise categories and products, and carefully plan merchandising promotions. We'll learn how, as one trade publication announced, grocers are switching tactics from an orientation on "the decadence of the '80s to a thrust towards value-pricing (where manufacturers compete to lower prices)." Consumers who understand these techniques have the ability to profit from them themselves.

• **Step Two** of the System involves using coupons, the most visible of the System's tools. I'll disclose the methods by which the Super Shopper acquires a cache of coupons. I'll demonstrate the importance of buying national-brand products and at the same time avoiding blind loyalty to particular brands. I'll outline a method for organizing coupons and for organizing effective and quick shopping trips.

• **Step Three**, refunding, is the heart of the System. You'll learn about the hidden value of bulk purchases, the sources of refund and rebate information, and the methodology of refunding—what I call the "refunder's SOS." I'll explain for you the three types of rebates and clarify the terminology used by refunders.

• **Step Four** is understanding the refunding network.

The network is the vital source of knowledge about the thousands of refund offers available at any given time. There are four methods by which refunders engage in swapping, and several ways in which swaps and refund information are discussed. Newsletters are critical tools for Super Shoppers; these inexpensive periodicals cement this network from which bargains and friendships develop.

• **Step Five** is the method by which refunders receive gifts, what manufacturers call "premiums," in the mail. Many refunders use this process to collect the gifts they then distribute over the holidays. These premiums include cereal-box gifts, clothing, computer game cartridges, stuffed animals, and cameras. You'll become knowledgeable about the various types of offers and their many advantages.

• **Step Six** of the System is a little-known but profitable way to earn direct cash for coupons. Here, I'll explain how people may legally sell their unused coupons to those who wish to use them. That network of dedicated couponers I mentioned earlier has established forums and carefully organized structures by which this trade is accomplished. Industrious coupon collectors can realize benefits equal to the savings they gain through combined couponing and refunding.

. . .

The Super Coupon Shopping System is designed for our value-conscious times. It can succeed in doing what one talk show host said of me in his introduction, "She never pays full price and she wants you to never pay full price." So go out there and make me look good.

Understanding the Retail Structure

---✂

Shopping is an American passion. In 1991 American consumers made retail purchases of almost two trillion dollars (that's a two followed by the number of zeros and commas usually reserved for discussions of the federal deficit). According to the *Progressive Grocer*'s 59th Annual Report, over 376 billion of those dollars were spent in grocery stores. This is not mom-and-pop business. In fact, the industry is big business, and getting bigger. Convenience stores and small local grocery stores account for only about one-quarter of all its sales. The remaining 75 percent of sales occur in supermarkets, individual stores where annual sales total at least two million dollars.

And the supermarket industry itself is becoming ever more consolidated into a small number of very large chains. Chain supermarkets earned over 70 percent of all supermarket dollars in 1991, completely dwarfing the sales of local "independent" supermarkets. The chains themselves are becoming dominated by a small number of heavy hitters.

There are over 30,000 supermarkets in the United States. Only five companies—American Stores, Kroger, Safeway, A & P, and Winn-Dixie—control over one-quarter of all the sales of these 30,000 supermarkets. These companies command enormous resources and use them for one primary purpose: to increase the number of consumer dollars flowing to their coffers.

Now this is not all bad for consumers. The industry remains competitive, and the concentration of money in the hands of some companies has led to sophisticated marketing approaches, which result in improved shopping experiences. Some of the large companies set standards that others must follow in order to survive.

Aside from competition among themselves, supermarkets are also affected by two other influences. One group, the manufacturers, has a strange relationship with the supermarket industry. They are dependent on one another, and yet they compete in two areas: access to the consumer and responsibility for marketing costs. This competition, as will be described later, leads to some very important consumer benefits.

The other influence is a relatively novel retailing development. Supermarkets have become terrified by what the industry calls mass merchandisers. These are warehouse stores, wholesale buying clubs, and discount stores such as Wal-Mart and Price Club. The industry's concern is reflected by the appearance in *Supermarket News*, a weekly trade publication, of a regular feature titled "Wal-Mart Watch." In that feature, Wal-Mart is described as being "perceived as the fastest growing and most formidable threat to retailers today." The pressures created by these merchandisers create special opportunities, described later, for Super Shoppers.

What Shoppers Want

There's a myth that shoppers are attracted to supermarkets by the relative quality of a store's produce and meat departments. The popularity of the myth is no doubt fueled by the common experience of entering a store to confront rows of glistening, colorful vegetables immediately followed by a neat, chilled array of freshly packaged cuts of meats. Well, these perishables departments may have their importance to consumers, but their locations in the store reflect retailers' needs. In an industry survey asking consumers to rank the importance of twenty store characteristics, the quality of the perishables departments failed to make consumers' top-five lists.

What shoppers want is comfort, value, and information. The top five qualities ranked by shoppers in *Progressive Grocer*'s 1992 survey were, in order, cleanliness, low prices, labeling of all prices, accurate and pleasant checkout clerks, and marking of freshness dates on products.

There's little mystery about the source of these needs. According to the Tax Foundation, only federal taxes and housing expenses swallow more of the family dollar than does food. Families spend *less* on such things as health care, state and local taxes, transportation, and recreation. With so much of their paychecks being left at the checkout counter, it's little wonder that shoppers are interested in the quality and cost of the products they purchase.

Shoppers' search for value is causing fundamental changes in the industry. A divisional manager for the second largest of the chain stores, Kroger Co., recently told the *Wall Street Journal,* "In thirty years in the business,

I've never seen such a state of change." The change with which he was concerned was one not highly favored by retailers: decreases in both product prices and consumer expenditures.

There are two reasons why prices have been forced down: (1) Manufacturers, finding consumers more loyal to price than to brand name, must focus on lower prices and on promotions to gain consumer allegiances; (2) Retailers, suddenly finding Wal-Marts or warehouse buying clubs sprouting up on every vacant lot, are driven to protect their share of the market by discounting prices. As a result, consumers have begun spending less money in supermarkets. In fact, in two consecutive year-long periods, beginning in early summer 1990, consumers spent less in supermarkets than they had in previous years.

It is also unsurprising that shoppers want to shop in a nice place. Family grocery shopping is still primarily done by women; in only 17 percent of the nation's families is a man the primary shopper. For most of these women, almost 60 percent, household responsibilities share demands on their time with full- or part-time jobs. The average two to three times a week shopping trips of about an hour's duration each are no longer leisurely affairs; they bite into time that becomes more precious with its scarcity. Clean, pleasant stores alleviate some of the stress and also usually signal efficient operations that will conserve some of the shopper's time.

Manufacturers: The Cult of Progress

Americans have been said to love progress but hate change. Manufacturers seem to strive to meet these contradictory goals through the creation of "new and improved" products that also manage to retain some familiar elements. Most important, though, is the creation of products.

New products flow from manufacturers in a constant deluge. One marketing service reported the creation of over 1,500 health and beauty aids and nearly 3,000 food items in the first eleven months of 1991. *New Product News,* a publication whose very existence indicates the magnitude of the phenomenon, noted the creation in every year since 1989 of over 12,000 grocery products that differed from existing products either fundamentally or by brand, flavor, color, or variety.

This progress doesn't come cheaply to the manufacturers. A 1990 study found the average cost of developing and marketing a new product to be $4.7 million. That doesn't even include the actual costs of production. These are investments that someone expects will pay off in a big way.

An example of the process was recently reported in *Adweek's Marketing Week.* The company that manufactures Kleenex built technologically advanced plants that permitted it to produce "premium" toilet paper at only two-thirds of the costs encountered by other manufacturers. Kleenex was able to lower its price for toilet paper and still make money. And what was the competitors' response to Kleenex? In areas where Kleenex tissue is not sold, four rolls of the competition's toilet paper sell for around $1.30. Where Kleenex is sold, the price of the same tissue is reduced to about 79 cents. Rather than abandon the market, competitors are reducing their prices by 40 percent. One can't help but wonder how much of that 40-percent reduction had been nothing but pure profit for years. And in a product market where annual sales total $2.6 billion, that kind of pure profit is a lot of profit.

Manufacturers: Retailers' Limits

Once a product is developed, the manufacturer faces the critical problem of placing the product where consumers can determine the product's utility. Supermarket shelves are already filled with over 25,000 different products; how then can they make room for another 12,000 every year? The only solutions are to expand total shelf space or to eliminate quantities or brands of other products.

Stores can expand only so much, and they've done a good deal of it lately. Stores shoehorned into tight urban areas have little or no expansion room available; much of the expanded shelf space comes from new construction, where stores average over 40,000 square feet (about the size of 200 normal living rooms strung together) and range beyond twice that area. Interestingly, much of the growth has not been at the loss of other, smaller stores; for about a decade, until 1991, the pace of supermarket openings outstripped the pace of closings. However, there are certainly finite limits to the amount of real expansion that can occur.

The primary form of shelf control occurs through two techniques, "delisting" and "slotting allowances," neither of which is wildly popular with affected manufacturers.

Delisting is the simple removal from the store of items that the store determines are selling too slowly. Many items fail to achieve consumer niches; between 80 and 90 percent of all new items fail in their first year of existence. Failure of items harms stores in ways beyond simple occupancy of otherwise productive shelf space. Inventory has to be handled, signs and price tags produced, warehouse space and workpower utilized, and data have to be entered and maintained. One chain estimated each of its stores used the equivalent of one employee working forty-two-hour weeks all year only to handle the extra work generated by new products.

As a result, delisting is taken quite seriously. Products are carefully monitored, and in some cases stores attempt to have manufacturers share the cost of product introduction to the store shelves by instituting "failure fees." These can be quite harsh. They require the manufacturer (or the vendor of its goods) to pay a certain sum to the retailer if a minimum amount of the product has not been sold in a fairly brief time period—usually ninety days. They also then require the vendor to remove, at its own cost, the remaining product from the retailer's warehouses within a shorter period—usually thirty days—or face the donation of the goods to a nonprofit agency at the vendor's cost. To vendors and manufacturers of failed goods, delisting and its associated costs clearly reflect the harsher edge of a supply-and-demand market system.

Almost universally accepted, and only slightly less disliked by manufacturers, are slotting allowances, which appear to have been introduced into the industry in the early 1980s. These are fees paid by vendors to compensate retailers for the costs of adding products to warehouse slots and store shelves. Suppliers who refuse to pay the fees don't get their products on the stores' shelves.

Retailers and suppliers differ over the effect of these fees. Retailers claim that the fees cover only a part of their costs, and suppliers fret that the fees really provide retailers with another source of profit. The fees can be extensive; a 1987 *Progressive Grocer* survey showed these fees reaching as much as $40,000 per item.

Consumers: Manufacturers' Allies?

It seems quite remarkable, another David slaying Goliath story, that huge multinational grocery product corporations can be held hostage to the demands of supermarkets. Part of the reason lies in the size of supermarkets, which, now dominated by large chains, have begun to approach the financial stature of those corporations.

More significant, though, are changes in the American marketplace. Consumers are savvier, aware that the proclaimed differences among many products go no deeper than their labels. The effectiveness of television advertising has diminished as the number of channels has increased. The audience that manufacturers once hoped to captivate by advertising on a particular network has shrunk dramatically in the last fifteen years.

Brand loyalty, that triumph of late-nineteenth-century marketing, has also declined. Part of the decline is due to decreasing advertising effectiveness, and part is due to the actions of manufacturers themselves. Consumers are overwhelmed by the onslaught of new products, many of which are some form of improvement upon the "perfect" products to which they have developed their loyalties. These constant changes and product introductions have led to cynicism on the part of some consumers that the only worthwhile loyalty is to low prices. Others, bombarded by the new products' claims of quality and novelty, try them and, as a result, don't attach themselves to any particular brands.

Manufacturers have ended up creating a vicious Catch-22 for themselves. Finding consumers motivated by price concerns, manufacturers have begun aggressively advertising value and offering significant money-saving promotions. As a result, consumer cynicism increases as they become unwilling to increase manufacturer profits by paying prices beyond those set during promotional discount offers. Manufacturer emphasis on value only enhances the already strong tendency toward price-consciousness on the consumer's part.

But with the increasing clout of retailers, manufacturers have an even greater need to establish bases of consumer loyalty. They not only need consumers to purchase their goods, but they need retailers to at least perceive consumer pressure to place the manufacturer's goods on the retailer's shelves where consumers will have access to them. This pressure is developed by fostering three attitudes among consumers: desire for the particular products, feelings of goodwill toward the manufacturer, and opportunities to save money at the manufacturer's expense.

Consumer desire is established through effective advertising and, to some extent, through innovative products of greater quality and utility. Goodwill is created through the manufacturer's responsiveness to complaints, by a consumer history of satisfaction with a product, and through various forms of giveaways. That's where we Super Shoppers come in, taking the savings but leaving the loyalty to those who can afford it. Money-saving opportunities occur principally through coupons and rebate offers, methods that manufacturers use in the hope of developing buying patterns that will establish the brand loyalty that protects their share of the market.

Manufacturers' Tools I: Realistic Imagining

Not that these manufacturing giants need to be pitied. They are still giants, and quite powerful ones at that. The Fortune 500 list of companies is dotted with the names of grocery producers such as Procter & Gamble, General Foods, and Campbell's Soups.

These companies did not join the nation's financial elite by simply rolling over when faced with competing demands. They fight back, either directly or through the influence of the consuming public. They continue to struggle with retailers by targeting the favor of the consumer, hoping that consumers will pressure retailers to carry their products.

Unfortunately, much of their attempt to gain consumer loyalty is accomplished through blue smoke and mirrors. After all, just how many times can a toothpaste or a laundry detergent become "new and improved"? Stuck in the belief that consumers expect products to constantly progress (an expectation produced by decades of "new and improved" advertising), manufacturers engage in what marketers call "realistic imagining." Consumers are enticed to see within a new item some familiar features of the old (the "realistic") and imagine the benefits added to those features by the new. Unfortunately, we remain gullible to these tricks.

The tricks have become more subtle than simply throwing on a "new and improved" label. In *Adweek*, Kevin Kerr noted how two similar shampoos received entirely different consumer receptions due to different marketing strategies. Both shampoos offered the innovation of combining shampoo and conditioner in one bottle. The first, Small Miracle, was marketed as the shampoo of the future. Our lack of familiarity with it indicates just how brief that future was. Advertising for the other, Pert Plus, emphasized the convenience of using a combined shampoo and conditioner. Pert Plus has gone on to become the best-selling shampoo in the nation.

Now, most of us are not dumb. We didn't need to have someone shampooing his or her hair on television directly tell us that a combined shampoo and conditioner would mean that we'd only have to use one product to shampoo and condition our hair. But apparently what we did need, at least for Pert Plus to succeed, was to have someone tell us that we really *desired* that convenience. Because once that desire was communicated to us, we *had* to have it. And that is the frightening power of advertising. Somehow need, always a difficult term to define (try reasoning with a three-year-old about why she doesn't really *need* that candy bar at the checkout counter), expands when someone tells us enough times, in pleasant enough ways, that it now includes things we'd never before even considered.

On the other hand, we're not complete suckers. Brand-name items are often of high quality. Although there may not be much difference between two nationally advertised automatic dishwashing detergents, the difference between those two and some discount brand may be the difference between clean dishes and dishes coated with a film of some congealed chemical. The big corporations do create quality products. What the savvy shopper has to do is decide which of those products is needed, discern the real differences among them, and, avoiding artificial loyalties, take advantage of the best bargains.

Manufacturers' Tools II: Satisfaction

Another tactic manufacturers employ is to get us to like them. Now they know that we're not going to get warm and fuzzy feelings about General Foods or Procter & Gamble or Beatrice. But Tony the Tiger, the Jolly Green Giant, and the Pillsbury Doughboy are characters of an entirely different stripe. We grew up with these creatures (and hundreds of others), and our children are growing up with them now too.

Granted, most of us are not going to buy products—at premium prices, no less—just because they're plugged by cartoon characters. But those characters soften the image of the corporations whose products are being pitched and help fragment our perceptions of those corporations. We begin to identify each product as a separate entity, based on its brand name or on some other element like a signature character. The product then looks unique, separate, and vulnerable to the efforts of competitors. It seems to need and deserve our loyalty. Of course, the truth is starkly the opposite. Almost every product on a grocery store's shelves was put there by a Fortune 500 company. And that company's real loyalty is to its stockholders.

But companies need to seem loyal and "good" to consumers, hoping that consumers will reciprocate that loyalty. So, having given us some kind of character or image about which we can feel comfortable, the companies give us some real actions by which we can measure their goodness.

In order to build goodwill, companies generally strive to (1) guarantee our satisfaction with the product; (2) respond readily and sympathetically to complaints; and (3) give away gifts, often emblazoned with the company name or symbol, but gifts nonetheless. To the unwary consumer, these things are balls and chains, linking them, loyally and forever, to the company providing them. To the savvy consumer, these things are what Creole-speaking

Louisianians call "lagniappe," something extra for free.

Probably the most cunning component of this trinity occurs through the development of product satisfaction. Somehow people are convinced that one cold remedy, differing from another only by name, does a better job of eliminating sniffles, or that one detergent with added bleach "out-whitens" another detergent with the same added bleach. But brand-name products differ from their cousins only superficially. The savvy shopper recognizes this and uses brands that benefit her, switching brands whenever it seems advantageous. She buys detergent to clean clothes, not to identify herself as a woman who uses Tide or All or Fab or any other brand. Satisfy yourself, not some company's profit margin.

The other two methods, corporate responsiveness and giveaways, do provide benefits to those very few consumers who use them, but without requiring that one swear loyalty to a brand name.

The major corporations all have set up fairly elaborate customer-service departments. These departments respond quite readily to customer complaints, compensating consumers for damaged or spoiled products with refunds, certificates for replacement products, and coupons—often at values exceeding the cost of the original defective item. And one of the advantages of this technological age is that this response can be achieved without so much as the cost of a postage stamp. Most companies have toll-free 800 phone numbers, often displayed on the products, for these customer-service departments.

Recognizing that it seems to be human nature to have a better memory for those things that went wrong than for what went right (especially when corporate advertising has created such a mythical sense of what is "right" in the brand-name world), these departments go to great lengths to assuage customers dissatisfied with their products. They are departments well worth using.

As we'll see later in this book, companies also simply give away a lot of things to those who know how to properly request their "gifts." What savvy shoppers have to remember is that the opportunity to receive these gifts was purchased with the product and requires no further obligation on their part. Just because your children get a baseball autographed by Tony the Tiger, it doesn't require them to eat Frosted Flakes every morning before they put on their baseball cleats. Savvy shoppers get what they can from these grocery corporations and give them no more than they have to.

Manufacturers' Tools III: Money for You

Manufacturers try not to operate in an information vacuum. Countless market-research surveys have shown them that consumers, not surprisingly, want to spend less money on their purchases. And manufacturers, who want to give consumers enough of what consumers desire so that their products are purchased, do compete with lower prices. Aware, though, that the second edge to the price-cutting blade is decreased profits, they try to give consumers only little nibbles at lower prices, nibbles they hope will lead shoppers onto the hook of brand loyalty. To gain this loyalty, the manufacturers have to create discounting gimmicks that consumers will recognize as flowing not from their local supermarket but from the creator of the products.

The two forms these gimmicks take are coupons and rebates. Consumers are enticed into purchasing products by the prospect of immediate coupon savings or the promise of cash refunds. Coupons with staggered expiration dates and rebate programs that require multiple purchases of a product provoke steady purchases of an item, a pocketbook loyalty that manufacturers hope will grow into habitual purchasing. Finally, the coupons and rebates, direct from the manufacturer, are presumed to establish consumer identification with the beneficent company providing these savings.

Well, much of this book is devoted to showing how consumers can use these programs to reap considerable rewards without becoming impaled on these manufacturers' hooks. What is important to remember about these incentive programs is that they offer consumers more powerful reasons to continue buying brand-name products while avoiding loyalty to specific brands.

Most rebate and coupon offers have specific, and ever-shortening, lifespans. The average manufacturer's coupon now expires within three months of the date it's issued. As few manufacturers continue coupon offers throughout the year, even avid collectors can realize year-round savings only by changing brands with the availability of coupon offers. But all coupon savers will realize savings unavailable to those who buy generic, store-brand, and discount-brand items, because, when the Super Shopping System is employed, coupon savings will result in lower prices overall than discount or generic prices. Plus, consumers gain the quality advantages found in the national-brand products.

Supermarkets: The Power in the Middle

Supermarkets have successfully turned their middle position, between consumers and manufacturers, from one of vulnerability to one of control. As Edward McLaughlin and Vithala Rao describe in *Decision Criteria for New Product Acceptance and Success,* manufacturers have lost much of their leverage in the marketplace. The constant struggle for limited supermarket shelf space has given retailers greater authority in setting the terms by which they accept the products that will fill those shelf spaces.

Increasingly, in fact, merchandisers are forced to take on responsibilities and risks traditionally handled by retailers. Manufacturers' representatives now often stock shelves and set up promotional displays. (Have you ever asked a supermarket "employee" for directions and been told "I don't work here"?) Manufacturers are also required to buy back unsold inventory and to ship smaller, more frequent deliveries of products, reducing the retailers' warehousing costs. These changes are all the result of retailers' growing muscle in the industry.

Fortunately for consumers, retailers can't quite apply the same muscle to them. The industry, although increasingly concentrated, is still quite competitive, with numerous stores romancing consumers for their dollars. So, while manufacturers may feel exposed to the iron fist, consumers, for the most part, feel only the velvet glove. The trick for consumers, of course, is to avoid being squeezed by that glove. And retailers are becoming ever more sophisticated in gently, and pleasantly, applying that squeeze.

Store Layout: The Exotic Bazaar

The entryway to the modern supermarket offers little hint that it is a place where people will shop for simple groceries. Most of the stores constructed in the last decade are what the industry calls "extended stores," with the extensions into product lines ranging from lawn furniture to bins of flavored coffee beans, products our parents never saw at the local A & P. These extended stores contain an array of seemingly independent departments, "boutiques" offering personalized services and unique products. They're designed to create the image of a bustling market filled with entrepreneurial farmers and peddlers right out of the pages of American mythology.

Which is fine, up to a point. Creating a fanciful marketplace can be fun. And while supermarkets do want their customers to have fun, what they want most is for that fun to include the expenditure of consumer dollars. Supermarket boutiques accomplish this goal in several ways.

These specialized little areas contain high-profit items like ready-to-eat hot foods, trays of salad-bar vegetables, and live trout ready to be selected and processed. The very busyness of these areas draws shoppers to them. The swirl of activity, combined with smells like the warm yeastiness of fresh bread or the tang of barbecue sauce convinces shoppers to buy products that were not in their minds when they picked up the car keys to head for the store. Just how many shopping lists are headed by "choose a live rainbow trout" or "two slices of supreme deluxe pizza"? These areas can slide shoppers down a slippery slope of impulse buying that a nicely written shopping list is unable to check.

The boutiques also succeed because of their location. Part of their ability to divert and entertain occurs because shoppers encounter them first. Time hasn't yet been expended in the store nor is there a full cart ominously indicating significant financial outlay. The shopper is still good-humored and, unknowingly, tremendously vulnerable.

This vulnerability is exploited. These boutique areas

seem chaotically inefficient, full of strange angular twists and turns that don't appear in the symmetrical aisles that make up the bulk of the store. It is, however, a very well-planned chaos.

Every twist is designed to turn the shopper toward another attractive display of some highly profitable product. These boutique areas usually include things like the retailer's "olde world" displays, delicacies that fetch premium prices and complement the fresh items sold in the boutique departments.

Usually this chaos ends by the time the shopper negotiates passage through these "service" and produce areas. Retailers recognize that most shoppers do want to get out of the store and get on with their lives. They also know that the longer a shopper is in the store, the more money the shopper spends.

Every extra minute spent roaming the aisles—or twisting around counters and displays—leads to an average of almost two dollars more spent in the store. So store planners front load this extra time, putting the obstacles in shoppers' paths early, when they are less likely to be annoyed by them. They also make maximum use of this time by filling these areas with those items from which retailers realize the greatest profits.

Into the Aisles: Displays and Prices

Retailers' tricks don't end with the mazes. All the neatly organized straight and wide aisles contain a host of pricing and display tricks of their own.

Every aisle has, at each end, "end-cap" displays where grocers stack pyramids of some product adorned with hand-lettered signs proclaiming a low price. Often, though, the price is a good deal higher than the prices of other brands of similar products. But the end-cap display entraps because it looks like a sale; also, by isolating the displayed product, it makes comparison pricing more difficult.

Within the aisles, displays are carefully calculated to gain the greatest sales and profits. The best-selling brand names of a product are placed vertically across the shelves at eye level. Either next to, or directly beneath, that brand will be placed the store brand, which is the most profitable to the retailer. Even the location of different-sized products is determined by profitability. Large economy-sized containers are placed on the lowest shelves, not out of aesthetic or structural considerations, but because retailers realize the least profit from these sizes and shoppers are least likely to pluck items from the lowest shelves.

Shoppers also need to be wary of cross-promotions of expensive and discounted items. For years retailers have been luring shoppers to their stores with "loss leaders," items priced so low that the store takes a loss in their sale, but makes up the loss by bringing in customers who purchase other products. Cross-promotions are sophisticated wrinkles in the concept of loss leaders.

A store will advertise a special event like an "Oktoberfest sale." The retailer might offer special, and deep, savings on sausages and buns. The sale items will then be located in a cluster of complementary products, like imported mustards, canned sauerkraut, paper plates and napkins, and sparkling grape juices, all of which will have decidedly non-sale prices. The retailer expects shoppers to supplement their sale purchases with enough of the other items so that the retailer will enjoy a tidy profit.

Stores continue to use pricing tactics that seem laughably simple but whose durability indicates their effectiveness. For some reason, odd-cent prices seem cheaper to us. It seems almost absurd in this day when pennies are literally given away (almost every convenience store and coffee shop has the "need one take one, have one leave one" penny cup at its cash register) that shoppers should feel that a 59-cent item is substantially cheaper than a 60-cent item, but we do. So markets keep pricing items to make us feel that we're getting a bargain.

Stores also use the technique of multiple-unit pricing to create the illusion of bargains. Often these package deals of "two-for" or "five-for" are deals only to the retailer trying to move a product sitting too long on the shelf. The actual unit price is often no less than was the single-item price.

The Electronic Caress

Although the existence of electronic checkout scanners was a revelation to the President of the United States in 1991, most ordinary shoppers have long acknowledged them as nice little gadgets speeding us through the tedium of the checkout line. But those innocent little scanners provide a good deal more service to their owners.

They provide information, some of it surprising. The scanners not only read the prices of items but also enter the sales of the items into the store's computer database. The store uses this information in some obvious ways, such as for monitoring and controlling its inventory. The information is also used in some large-scale and in some very personal ways.

Many stores across the country feed this scanner information to a Chicago organization, Information Resources, Inc., which analyzes it to determine marketing trends and consumer interests. Every week, this organization is given data on 45 million different product purchases in the country. This immense and almost instantaneously updated base of information provides manufacturers and retailers with a staggering ability to track demographic shopping patterns.

More personal is the information supermarkets can compile about individual shoppers. Many stores with scanners also utilize systems where shoppers, in order to write checks or to receive certain discounts, must swipe special magnetically encoded cards through machines at the checkout counter. Shoppers receive the cards only after filling out forms, forms that provide the store with another database that can be used in conjunction with the information compiled from the checkout scanners.

The store's computers can then easily track the personal buying patterns of whole classes of people, based on the information contained in the forms and monitored by the purchases made by them while using the encoded cards. They can also track individual buying habits and then target specific people for promotions to which they would be most receptive, such as sending coupons for greeting cards to someone who buys cut flowers.

The cards are also used to enter electronic coupon savings without requiring the trouble of clipping paper. Some stores have entirely replaced store coupons with discounts subtracted from the shopper's bill after the card is run through the machine. Others have also begun similar credits with selected manufacturer offers.

Stores also have begun installing automatic coupon machines at checkout counters. These machines dispense coupons to people whose purchases indicate receptiveness to the coupon, such as providing a coupon for Pampers to someone who has just purchased Luvs or Huggies disposable diapers.

Electronics have also invaded the shopping aisles. Some stores have prototype shopping carts which, when they pass sensors in the aisles, activate recorded messages exhorting customers on the virtues of nearby products. More common are coupon dispensers in the aisles, blinking red lights that draw customer attention to immediate 35-cent savings that might create the impulse to purchase a product otherwise passed by.

Finally, supermarkets have begun adding another convenience for shoppers, which has the convenient—to retailers—effect of increasing customer expenditures: They've begun accepting credit cards.

Between 1991 and 1992, the number of supermarkets accepting Visa and MasterCard skyrocketed from about 800 to over 8,000. The increase was spurred by the stores' growing technological capability and by the credit card companies lowering the processing rate charged to the stores. The danger for consumers is that credit purchases somehow seem less real than cash purchases, and so it becomes much easier to buy things on impulse. In fact, a 1991 MasterCard survey found that customers shopping with credit cards spent six dollars more during each supermarket shopping trip than they did when paying in cash.

The Shopper's Tools

The most potent tool shoppers have is the opportunity to choose. The great consumer advantage to living in a market economy is that there are competing suitors vying for our money and attention. The primary pitfall awaiting consumers is restriction of that choice, a restriction each of those suitors wants made in its favor.

Alert consumers can use the struggles of corporate giants to their benefit. Supermarkets, losing ground to discount stores, respond by lowering some prices and jazzing up their stores. Manufacturers, buffeted by diminished advertising strength and increased retailer muscle, have to more directly court the consumers of their products. Supermarkets and manufacturers, in their efforts to benefit their own self-interests, create opportunities for consumers to save money.

But manufacturers and retailers are far from impotent. Both are busy creating new tools and methods by which to increase their profitability. Consumers must remember that such profitability always comes at the consumer's expense. Step One of the Super Shopping System, which is summarized in the following points, is the process by which consumers become aware of their ability to save money at the supermarket.

Step-One Summary

1. **Be loyal to yourself.** Slavish adherence to a particular brand benefits only the manufacturer of that brand. Unless you really discern specific benefits in a particular product, be willing to switch products. Often the differences between name brands extend only to their names.

   The same standard applies to stores. Your power lies in your ability to choose where to spend your money. Don't let mindless habit give some corporation this power by default. Shop in the stores that give you what you want. Remember that you're dealing with big business here.

2. **Prepare for your shopping trips.** Read the advertising circulars *before* you shop. Learn what's on sale where. Pay attention to the discount stores. Clip coupons and take advantage of shopper discount programs. If there are benefits to having magnetically encoded store cards, get them.

3. **Use a shopping list.** If you enter a modern supermarket without a list, you might leave without any money. The store is filled with sophisticated lures and detours. Try to stick to the list.

4. **Stay alert.** Don't buy "bargains" unless you're sure they really are bargains. Watch out for large displays that are isolated from similar items. Be careful where complementary products are clustered. Compare prices carefully; don't be misled by package deals.

5. **Don't buy what you don't need.** Try to reach your own definition of what products are important to you. Don't buy bargains simply because they're bargains. Money spent on items you don't use, regardless of how discounted the price, is still money wasted.

6. **Have fun.** You have to shop anyway, so try to enjoy it. The modern supermarket, if you understand its layout, can be negotiated fairly easily. Checkout is faster due to scanners. All the gimmicks and free samples can be pleasant as long as you don't let them induce you into spending money you don't really want to spend.

Coupons: Shopping for (Almost) Free

--- ✂

I t seems that most Americans can't quite decide what to do about coupons. On the one hand, almost everyone makes at least occasional use of them. Yet fewer than four out of every hundred distributed are actually used.

Surveys consistently show coupon use to be largely unrestricted by income categories. A recent survey by one of the companies that acts as a clearinghouse for redeeming coupons found that almost 75 percent of people earning over $50,000 supplemented their wages with coupon savings. And the rate of use was even greater for those with lower incomes.

The great majority of these couponers, though, use fewer than five coupons a week. In fact, concentrated coupon use is so rare that the industry classifies "heavy users" as those who do use five coupons a week.

Well, five coupons a week is a good deal less than the Super Coupon Shopping System shopper uses. I'll use five coupons for just one family lunch.

For the most part people seem to treat coupons as just bits of loose change, unworthy of their time and effort. Super Shoppers know, however, that a bit of time and some disciplined organization can lead to quite substantial savings.

It's a process that can also be fun. There was a time, as little as ten years ago, when couponers were seen as somewhat daffy, obstructionist shoppers, tying up checkout lines while they fumbled through piles of creased little papers. Things have changed.

For one thing, years of economic recession have led to an appreciation of all money-saving schemes. For another, couponing has received a lot of favorable press. As I mentioned in the Introduction, I've appeared on hundreds of television shows demonstrating the Super Shopping System. And periodicals as unexpected as the *American Legion Magazine* now write articles extolling the virtues and relative ease of couponing.

And couponers are less likely to be obstructionist. Many, especially those who practice couponing in a large-scale manner, arrive at the checkout counter well organized and present their coupons as readily as they do their cash (what little of it they have to use). Technology also helps. Most coupons are now printed with universal product codes on their faces, identifying the couponed product and the discounted amount. Cashiers need only run the coupons across their scanners, allowing even a thick sheaf to be processed rapidly.

There is a definite pleasure in watching negative numbers fly across the face of the cash register as the coupons are scanned. It is a pleasure that culminates in the very real satisfaction of seeing a very real and very immediate reduction in my grocery bill. There's a special satisfaction in wheeling away grocery carts containing products for which I've paid less than half the price.

I'm not the only person who does this; in fact I don't even hold the record for the best trip. A New Jersey bus

Typical cash-off coupons

driver, Kenneth Schnoorfisch, is legendary for using coupons to acquire, in one trip, $869.79 worth of groceries for which his cash outlay was a total of $2.16 in taxes. Thousands of other shoppers save at least 10 to 20 percent of their weekly grocery bills with limited time invested in organizing and using coupons.

Coupons are just one part of the System; they establish a base, but the true Super Shopper will not settle for a mere 10- to 20-percent savings. That kind of saving is only the System's starting point.

Their Number and Objectives

Since 1980 the number of coupons distributed in the United States has just about doubled every five years, so that by 1992 almost 400 billion coupons were distributed. It's not as if these scraps of paper were simply good for a few pennies off the price of an item. NCH Promotional Services, Inc., a leading clearinghouse for coupon redemption, estimated that the average face value of these coupons was just over 50 cents. That's paper, then, worth almost $200 billion, not exactly loose change.

Manufacturers distribute all this value for a variety of reasons beyond the obvious provision of an incentive to immediately buy their products. Coupons are one of the most important tools used in new-product introductions. Manufacturers don't want to introduce new products at temporary, reduced prices because consumer resistance to increasing the price would effectively derail the product. Instead, the product is introduced at its regular shelf price, but heavy coupon promotions are offered, which may virtually halve the product's price. It's a beneficial strategy; a truism in the industry is that the most effective product introduction occurs by combining distribution of free samples of a new product with a coupon for the product.

Coupons are also used to protect or strengthen an established product's share of the market. Usually, their purpose is to steal customers away from other brands, encouraging some brand switching and hoping to turn the triers of the product into newly loyal customers. Interestingly, loyal brand users tend to be among the smallest users of coupons. Coupons seem to be a promotional concept that is designed not to reward loyal users but primarily to capture new users.

Coupons also help manufacturers in their struggle to place products on supermarket shelves by orchestrating customer clamor for certain products. Strong coupon promotions lead to customer inquiries about products, and retailers are mindful of such requests. In addition, when coupons for a product start turning up in great numbers, the retailer knows there is strong manufacturer support for the product.

Primarily, though, coupons let manufacturers fight for market share by reducing prices without actually acknowledging the reduction. Manufacturers know that today's consumer has a heightened value consciousness. Yet manufacturers hate to reduce prices for even temporary periods because of consumer resistance to later increases. Coupons are the safest way for manufacturers to offer sale prices.

Where to Find Coupons

Manufacturers' coupons are often called "cash-offs," in recognition of what they offer: cents off the purchase of specified products. One of the nice features of these cash-offs (aside from their value) is that other people go through all the effort of getting them to you. Manufacturers want these things in your hands in the hope that you'll use them to put the manufacturers' products in those same hands.

FSIs in the Sunday Paper

Over three-quarters of all cash-offs are distributed in glossy free-standing inserts (FSIs) in the Sunday papers. To uninitiated shoppers these FSIs are just more garbage of a particularly inconvenient type because of the need to specially sort them for recycling efforts. To Super Shoppers FSIs can be a primary reason to not only buy the Sunday paper but to scrounge through recycling bins for discards.

In fact, such recycling bins can be a real gold mine. A friend who lives in a Florida co-op and knows of my penchant for couponing and of the household needs generated by my four sons recently sent me, courtesy of her recycling bin, 96 coupons for free trial-size containers of a new Fab liquid detergent product. Over a period of some weeks, I cashed them all in and received about thirty dollars' worth of free detergent. I can guarantee you that my boys' clothes never look cleaner to me than when I can launder them for free.

Within Newspapers and Magazines

Another, more modest, source lies within the pages of newspapers and magazines. Within the ordinary pages of the papers, nestled between news stories and normal advertisements, are what the industry calls ROP solos (for right on the page, and solo because no other coupons appear on the page). These usually appear on the "food day" of the local papers, when the local stores distribute their advertising circulars in the paper. Food day usually comes right in the middle of the week.

Within the stores' advertising circulars, which are usually separate supplements inserted within the paper, is a different form of coupon, issued by the stores. These "in-ad" coupons are usually limited to use in the store offering them and usually have a very short redemption period, expiring upon distribution of the next week's circular. One critical, and quite popular, feature of these in-ads is that they can be used in conjunction with manufacturer cash-offs, increasing the shopper's savings.

Magazines are also a source of coupons. The best sources are the "women's" magazines, such as *Family Circle, Woman's Day, McCall's,* and *Ladies' Home Journal,* usually displayed near the checkout counter. But coupons can also be found in more general-interest magazines, some of which, like *Reader's Digest,* at times advertise on their covers the value of the coupons found within.

Of course, one shouldn't subscribe to racks of magazines just to acquire coupons, but they can be acquired from friends' discarded copies or through trades with friends. My neighbor Claire gives me her cereal coupons, and I give her the coffee coupons I find.

Another source of magazine coupons is the stacks of magazines in doctors' and dentists' offices. They don't clip them out, and I figure I might as well use the time in the waiting room gaining some profit.

Home Mailers

There are generally two types of home mailers: the envelopes addressed to "occupant" sent out by large marketing companies, and directly addressed envelopes mailed out by manufacturers and their representatives. To some people these mailers are "junk" mail destined for the recycling bin. For Super Shoppers, the contents of these envelopes are to be recycled back to the manufacturer.

In-Store Coupons

One of the most direct ways manufacturers use to try to develop customer loyalty is "bounce-back" coupons. Coupons are printed on a package or inserted in the package for customers to use on a subsequent purchase of the same product. A smart shopper considers the added value of these bounce-backs when comparing the prices of products, deciding whether the prospective savings offered by these coupons helps justify the current price.

Manufacturers also use hang-tags, coupons draped around the necks of bottles or stuck on with removable adhesive to the sides of packages. These coupons are designed to be used immediately at the checkout counter.

Some stores also have dispensers in the aisles that emit coupons for products near the dispensers, intended for use on that day's purchases. There are also dispensers in some stores at the checkout lines, offering coupons for products either complementary to or competitive with those just purchased and read by the checkout scanner. The Super Shopper accepts and collects every useful coupon proffered, but *only uses them after determining that they provide the best possible value.*

The Select Coupon Program

While newspapers, magazines, home mailers, and store promotions provide a large quantity of coupons, they may not supply enough of the specific product coupons a shopper wants to use weekly. Realizing this problem, I set out to remedy the situation. The result was the formation of the Select Coupon Program. The main purpose of the Program is to provide coupons that shoppers can't find through their normal channels. We gather tremendous quantities of coupons from suppliers throughout the country who cut coupons from their magazines and local newspapers and sell them to the Select Coupon Program (see "Step Six: The Select Coupon Program"). Now shoppers in Des Moines, Denver, Peoria, and Oklahoma City, or any community where coupons are scarce have the option of finding their specific coupons. The Program inventories millions and millions of sorted and categorized national-brand cash-off coupons consisting of close to 1,000 selections. The Program's membership exceeds 100,000 shoppers. If you would like to receive information about the Select Coupon Program, send a business-size self-addressed stamped envelope to: Select Coupon Program, Box 338C, Tuckahoe, NY 10707.

Keeping Coupons Under Control

Coupons are so readily available that novice couponers find collecting relatively free of difficulty. Sheets of them might be culled from newspapers, Carol Wright mail packets salvaged from the junk-mail pile, and coupons of varying size clipped from magazines. The real difficulty lies in trying to decide what to do with all these pieces of paper. There will be a strong desire to stuff all this paper in a kitchen drawer or to tuck it behind some cans on a shelf. *Don't.* Out of sight is not only out of mind, but here it also means money out of your pocket. To keep the money in your pocket, this paper has to be handled with some form of organization.

Organization is, I know, a terrible word to many Americans. It conjures up images of faceless bureaucrats, totalitarian governments, or, worst of all, childhood memories of parental commands to "clean up this mess!" It's not that bad. In fact, organization can be the key to the independence with which we like to identify. Also, it's not that hard to accomplish, as long as the process is taken one step at a time.

Initial organization of coupons is not as daunting as the clutter of material might suggest. Keep in mind three points. First, remember that these are more than mere scraps of paper; these coupons are cash-offs, money in your pocket worthy of a little effort. Second, the organizational skills required are pretty trivial, barely rising beyond the ability to alphabetize. Third, because the task is somewhat tedious, you can occupy yourself simultaneously with something that provides entertainment without requiring much attention. So, it's worth money, it's simple, and you can watch television while you're doing it.

"It" is a filing system that works. All it requires is a suitable storage container and a method of dividing the space within the container.

There is no one perfect container. Some people use wonderful old pigeonhole desk hutches and mail sorters. Others are content with thumbtacking their coupons to cork bulletin boards. Most couponers, recognizing the benefits to portability, use either envelopes, coupon wallets, or index-card file boxes. I keep my cash-offs in three cardboard, accordion-style, business-size envelopes secured with rubber bands.

The best systems use containers that are small (because where there's space to throw things around, things get thrown around, usually in great disorder); portable (for transporting to the market and so that filing can be done where convenient); expandable (new couponers can be stunned by the share of each year's 400 billion coupons arriving in the hands of the alert, and can find too-modest systems quickly overrun); and durable (because Super Shoppers use their coupons...a lot).

I recommend using some kind of stout envelopes or wallets, file-card boxes, or a combination of envelope/wallet and boxes. Whichever type of container is used must be divided in some fashion, using labeled index cards, sheets of paper, or index dividers. Otherwise, the growing mass of coupons simply becomes too difficult to sift through, no matter how nicely it was alphabetized.

A Workable Filing System: The Categories

The purpose of the filing system is, of course, not just having a place in which to store the coupons, but, most importantly, gaining easy access to them. The basis of such access is the creation of simple categories.

The initial setup of these categories is worthy of some time and consideration, because people seem to find it quite difficult to alter systems once they've begun using them; instead they adapt the system to meet immediate needs. Such adaptations can result in wildly idiosyncratic structures, which are fine as long as the individual using the coupons is always idiosyncratically consistent. An example is a coupon for 35 cents off a tube of Pillsbury refrigerated chocolate chip cookie dough. The coupon could reasonably be filed under "Dairy Products" (because the product is found in the dairy cases of stores), under "Baked Goods," or under "Baking Supplies." It doesn't really matter under which category the coupon is filed; it does matter that you always know which category that will be. Make your system personal, but make it useful by following a few simple guidelines.

First, base your system on *product* categories. Don't create categories based on brand names. There are so many different brands that the file container would be overrun with divider cards. I alphabetize my coupons by brand name *within* product categories (so, "Paper Goods" would have coupons arranged: Bounty Paper Towels, Charmin Toilet Paper, Kleenex Tissues, etc.) without separating these coupons by dividers. Others find that just filing everything within a category in no particular order does an adequate enough job.

Next, choose categories that are tailored to the kinds of coupons that you will use. Make the categories specific enough that you won't have to sift through dozens of coupons to find each of the coupons you want to use on the day's shopping trip. If there are some products that your family uses often, then create a special category for those products. There are also products, like breakfast cereals, cleaning supplies, paper and plastic products, toiletries, and medicines, for which many coupons are printed. If you use some of the products in these broad categories more often then others, such as children's cereals, for example, then file those coupons separately from others in the product group.

Finally, once you've chosen category names, be certain to clearly and completely label the category dividers. Don't trust that you'll remember—and agree with—the reasoning that led you to once file one product under the heading of some broadly related product. If you intend to file

refrigerated dough coupons in the dairy category, then
write it on the divider.

Below is a list of product categories useful for organizing coupons. The outline form of the list indicates general
categories that may be broken down into subcategories or
simply left whole. Some of the categories may be combined into others, according to preference, as I've noted in
brackets:

Baby Supplies
  Disposable Diapers
Baking Supplies
  Packaged Mixes
Breads and Baked Goods
Canned Goods
  Canned Fruits and Vegetables
  Meats, Stews, Pastas
  Peanut Butter and Jellies
  Soups
  Tomato Sauces
Cereal
  Adult
  Children's
  Bran
  Hot Cereal
  Low-Sugar
Cleaning Supplies and Pesticides
Coffee, Tea, and Related Supplies
Condiments
  Ketchup
  Mayonnaise
  Mustard
  Oils

Pickles
Relish
Salad Dressings
Salsa
Shake 'n Bake
Dairy Products
  Cheese and Milk
  Margarine
  Refrigerated Doughs
  Yogurt
Dish Detergent [could be com-
  bined with Cleaning
  Supplies]
Dry Beverages
  Cocoa
  Milk Flavorings
  Milk Powder
Frozen
  Desserts and Ice Cream
  Dinners
  Pizza
  Potatoes
  Vegetables
  Waffles

Hardware
  Batteries
  Film
  Light Bulbs
  Miscellaneous
Juices: Canned and Frozen
Laundry Supplies [could be
  combined with Cleaning
  Supplies]
Meat [could be combined with
  Produce]
Medicines
  Adult
  Children
  Cold and Allergy Remedies
Paper Goods
  Facial Tissue
  Napkins
  Paper Towels
  Personal Supplies
  Toilet Paper
  Wraps and Plastic Bags
Pasta, Rice, Popcorn, Boxed

Dinners
Produce
Shampoo [could be combined
  with Toiletries]
Snacks
  Candy and Fruit Snacks
  Chips, Nuts, and Pretzels
  Cookies, Crackers, and
  Granola Bars
Soap [could be combined with
  Toiletries]
Soft Drinks
Toiletries
  Deodorant
  Lotions
  Shaving Supplies
Toothpaste
  Dental Floss
  Mouthwash [could be com-
  bined with Toiletries]
  Toothbrushes
Rainchecks
Restaurants

The actual process of filing can be approached in either of two ways. The first is to simply file coupons as they are garnered. This works fine for cash-offs clipped from magazines, received in the mail, or otherwise acquired in small numbers.

The second approach is to set aside a half hour or so a week during which coupons are filed. This method has become especially more suitable with the prevalence of free-standing inserts, where fairly large numbers of coupons are distributed in one packet and where some time has to be spent in clipping the cash-offs from the pages. Many shoppers find it helpful to do this clipping and filing just before they prepare their shopping lists, as it facilitates the use of the coupons.

An important point to remember about coupons is that most cash-offs are printed with expiration dates (EDs), which are strictly enforced. The number of coupons printed with EDs has grown in the last few years, perhaps as a balance against the overall increase in distributed coupons. In 1986, over 25 percent of coupons had no expiration dates. Today, fewer than 1 percent of all printed cash-offs are of this "evergreen" type. Now over half of all cash-offs will expire within three months of their issue, most (over 93 percent) are good for only six or fewer months.

While EDs can certainly cause disappointment, they also serve a housekeeping function. They keep collections from growing unusably bulky by prompting shoppers to either use or discard them. As new coupons are filed, expired ones should be culled and those nearing expiration pulled for use on the next shopping trip. Some people find it helpful to file all new coupons in the back of each category, so that as they select coupons they will be more likely to use those with earlier EDs.

EDs often follow cyclical patterns. Many expire at the ends of the year's quarters, with December 31 especially common. Other common dates are the last days of any month and two weeks to a month following the end of a season or holiday for which special products are used, such as candy at Halloween or cold and flu medications in the winter. Some couponers accent the EDs by circling or highlighting them.

Shoppers need to show some caution in clipping

coupons so that the EDs are left exposed on the face of the coupon. Checkout clerks must use these dates to determine if coupons are still valid, because the UPCs, encoded on most coupons, are not designed to provide expiration information through the electronic scanners. Checkers are required to personally verify the validity of cash-offs passing through their lines.

Planning the Shopping Trip:
Combine, Combine, Combine

Effective coupon use begins by remembering some points from Step One of the System. The most important is to keep in mind that you're shopping for the benefit of *you*. So, don't buy what you don't need, and watch out for all the ploys meant to distract you. Recall that your best defense against those distractions is to be prepared, preferably with a well-organized list. You're on a mission; stay on it.

Couponing success then follows by pursuing two tactics. One, buy name brands. Buy name brands because these are the products for which you have coupons (and, probably, rebate offers), and, obviously, you can't succeed at couponing without coupons. To the unorganized, however, this is not so obvious. Store-brand prices *are* cheaper than name brands. The trick lies in having accumulated and organized enough coupons so what you compare are the shelf prices of store brands with the discounted prices of name brands.

The other tactic is to combine, combine, combine. There are three types of store discounts that, when combined with coupons, can dramatically increase coupons' value:

1. Store sales. Stores have sales, which, of course, they advertise. The knowledge you can gain from these sale advertisements can be transformed easily into powerful savings. Before shopping, gather advertising circulars from all the stores at which you might shop. Make lists of the sale items your family uses. Check your coupon file to see if you have coupons for any of the sale products. Determine if the potential savings justify trips to the store(s). If they do, buy all of the sale items for which you have coupons and storage space. Whatever you buy now, you won't be forced to consider purchasing later, when you don't have coupons. Some people, though, do get carried away. It seems that especially men who become couponers also become great accumulators. I've heard horror stories of laundry detergent hoards so vast that the laundry room had no room for laundry. (The hoarder was cured when it was suggested that any future such caches would have to be stored in the garage, home to someone's workshop.)

Occasionally, you'll go to a store, having gone to all this trouble, armed with your list and coupons, only to find the store is out of the sale items. When this happens, request rainchecks. These are forms that permit you to purchase up to a certain quantity of the sale item at the sale price once the store has restocked the item. Many stores put expiration dates of one month on these forms; some have no expiration dates. Some stores will further decrease the sale price of items for which they give rainchecks as indicators of their good-faith efforts to fully stock their sale items.

2. Store coupons. These are printed by individual stores and are valid at only the store or chain that issues them. They usually appear in the weekly advertising circulars and in local newspapers. Stores often use these coupons to entice people into shopping at their markets. As a result, these coupons frequently offer substantial discounts, especially when combined with manufacturers' cash-offs.

Because of the statement on cash-offs, that only one coupon may be used for each item purchased, many shoppers assume that they cannot use both a manufacturer's and a store coupon for the purchase of the same item. That is an assumption that is as wrong as it is costly to the shopper. Such statements restrict only the *number* of manufacturers' coupons that can be used for each item. The restriction does not apply to store coupons, which are simply another way for the retailer to offer sale prices on products. As with sale items, shoppers should request rainchecks for store coupon items that are not in stock.

The bonanza provided by store coupons is not unchecked. Although the limitations vary from store to store, there are four restrictions that are quite common.

First, the coupons are valid only at the store or chain issuing them. Occasionally, a store will advertise its acceptance of competitors' coupons, but this is a marketing practice rarely found in the supermarket industry. Second, the coupons are usually valid only for the week in which they are issued. Third, the coupons, unlike store sale prices, tend to strictly limit the number of items that can be purchased. Finally, shoppers are usually required to make minimum purchases, ranging from five to ten dollars, before benefiting from these promotions.

All these restrictions are driven by the unique nature of these store coupons. Because the coupons substantially lower the price of the products, demand for the promoted product tends to be high. And while retailers may well suffer a loss from sales of the promoted items, they intend to recoup that loss through other sales in the store.

Some stores have eliminated paper coupons, replacing

them with special savings, still listed on the advertising circular, given to members of the store's shopping "clubs." The special savings are recorded on the customer's register tally when the customer swipes her club card through an electronic reader. Club membership is usually free and available to anyone who fills out the required form.

3. Double (or triple) coupons. Some stores, usually in highly competitive areas, offer double or, very rarely, triple manufacturers' coupons. The store simply multiplies the face value of the coupons by the stated amount.

Doubling is the sort of promotion that retailers hate. Because so many people use coupons (though not very effectively), doubling draws shoppers to stores so well that once one store offers the promotion, others are compelled to respond in kind. Once started, stores find this kind of promotion one that they can't halt very gracefully; all those customers who use their one to four coupons a week will be very aware of the decreased savings when the promotion ends.

Shoppers, and especially Super Shoppers, *love* doubled coupons. When retail representatives address refunding conventions, they are routinely greeted by chants of "DOUBLE COUPONS." Doubled coupons, especially in combination with store coupons or sale prices, often gain Super Shoppers products for which they pay *no* money. And free products are by far the best products.

Most stores, unfortunately, set some limitations on the use of doubled coupons. Some of the most common are:

• Limiting (usually two to four) the number of identical coupons doubled per customer.

• Limiting doubling to coupons valued at under one dollar.

• Refusing to double coupons for certain items—

such as coffee, alcohol, and cigarettes.

• Placing a limit on the total value of doubled coupons per shopper, such as limiting doubling to half the value of groceries purchased.

It's a good idea to check with the customer-service area of your store to learn what restrictions, if any, are placed on doubled coupons. You may find that there are no restrictions, as some stores do offer unlimited double coupons.

Planning the Shopping Trip: The List

You've probably waited impatiently in a shopping line somewhere while a customer ahead of you fumbled through a disorderly sheaf of coupons searching for those to present to the clerk. Or maybe you've seen someone in a store aisle frustratedly fanning a mass of coupons while comparing item prices to determine which offers the better value. You don't want to be one of those people, and if you follow the Super Coupon Shopping System, you won't be.

With the System, almost everything is organized in the relative comfort of your own home. Start by gathering pencil, paper, store advertising circular, and your coupon file. I keep all these items in one kitchen drawer that is devoted exclusively to couponing.

Look through the sale circular and write down products for which the store is providing its own coupons and products that are on sale, noting the sale prices and any size restrictions while trying to list the items in an order that approximates the layout of products in the store. Then fill out the list with other products that you need.

Next, search your coupon file for coupons that apply to these products. On your list, next to each product, note the value of any cash-offs you've found using a symbol to indicate that you have a coupon for the product. For non-sale products list the values of coupons that you have for various brands. Add to this list any coupons due to expire soon that you may decide to use.

One important point is to try to get the most product for the least money. Here, the Super Shopper will often use a strategy contrary to that used by ordinary shoppers. Most shoppers have learned that large economy sizes of products tend to cost a few pennies per ounce less than smaller-size products. With coupons, however, the opposite is often true. Because coupons reduce the absolute price of an item, regardless of size, the per-ounce savings are increased for smaller-size items.

For example, assume you have a coupon worth 50 cents on Joy, where a 22-ounce bottle costs $1.29 and a 32-ounce bottle costs $1.79. To the ordinary shopper, the 32-ounce bottle is about one-quarter of a cent an ounce cheaper than the smaller bottle, a savings of about eight cents. Using the coupon, though, makes the smaller bottle half a cent an ounce cheaper, saving the coupon shopper nine cents. But the Super Shopper waits to use her coupon until the detergent is placed on sale by the retailer (which happens frequently with name brands). The 22-ounce size might then retail for 79 cents; the Super Coupon Shopper happily picks it up for just 29 cents, which is, ounce for ounce, $1.07 less than the large "economy" size.

It is wise to also be alert to "trial size" offerings by manufacturers, miniaturized versions of products being introduced. Not only are the packages cute, but coupons usually result in these products costing nothing. Cute *and* free is a pretty nice combination.

Your shopping list may look something like this:

Bananas .29#
Apples * (.75 w/ Cheerios)
Salad greens
Potatoes
Crest 6.4 oz .79 *.50
Shampoo:
　Agree *.75
　Suave *.35 16 oz+
　Finesse *.50
Sun Light 22 oz .89 *.25x2
Laundry detergent:
　All *.50 64 oz+
　Era *.75
　Cheer *.50
Ragu Sauce 2/1 *.25x4
Breakfast Cereal:
　Kix *.75
　Kellogg's Corn Flakes *.50 20 oz+
　Rice Krispies *.35
Chips Ahoy Cookies *.75
Hershey's Assorted Miniatures *.45
Milk *(.75 w/ Frosted Flakes)
Minute Maid O.J. 12 oz .79
Ore-Ida Potatoes *.35
Charmin 4-pack .89 *.25/2

This list shows that the Minute Maid was on sale and that you had no matching coupons for it (because you show a sale price and no coupon symbol). The fruit and milk could be discounted by purchasing certain cereals and redeeming coupons. The Crest, Sun Light, Ragu, and Charmin are all sale items that can be combined with coupon savings (sale price and coupon symbol [*] and discount listed). No shampoo, detergent, or cereal is advertised on sale; nevertheless, you have a variety of coupons for these products and should be able to realize some savings (only coupon symbols and prices listed). The cookies, candy, and Ore-Ida products are not on sale, but you have coupons due to expire and will consider their purchase if the reduced price is right. The Suave, All, and Corn Flakes coupons are size-restricted (size listed after coupon symbol and price). You have multiple coupons for Sun Light and Ragu (coupon price followed by x and number of coupons). The Charmin coupon requires that you purchase two packages of the product (coupon price followed by / and number needed to purchase).

This type of list is not at all difficult to compile once you've developed a simple coding system similar to the one above. The information it provides permits you to easily determine the best values on products so that you get what you need at the best price in the least amount of time.

In the Store

Bring to the store your list *and* your coupons. Some people put into a separate envelope all the coupons they are considering using during their trip (determined when they compiled their list) and also bring with them the rest of their coupons. While shopping they separate usable coupons from those that won't be used, either because the store lacks the item or because even with the coupon discount the price is too high. I just bring my main storage envelope along with my list. As I shop and find the products for which I will use coupons, I move the coupons from their category compartments to the front of the file.

Much of my shopping over the years has been done in the company of one or more of my four sons. Using coupons has actually helped make the experiences fun, distracting, and even educational for them. Numerous times they've sat in the cart, earnestly scanning the aisles for the Joy or Cheer carton that matches the words and colors of a coupon. As they've gotten older they've helped work out item costs, taking great pride in flourishing their arithmetical skills. As a former elementary school teacher, I know that these are the kinds of experiences that really enhance children's education. As a mother, I know that a child happily helping me shop makes the task a lot more pleasant than one who spends the time sulking and whining about the boredom of the process.

Beyond providing educational entertainment for my children, the main reason to bring the coupon file on shopping trips is to have coupons ready for unadvertised specials for which coupons can be combined. For example, recently after the winter holidays, my local market put at the end of an aisle several shopping carts containing holiday candy marked down by half. I found several 9-ounce bags of Hershey's Kisses (wrapped in red and green foil) reduced to 75 cents. Using 35-cents-off coupons, doubled by the store, I got each of the bags for a nickel. Savings like this are good reason to have coupons organized and accessible: It would be a bit ridiculous to go shopping while lugging about a cork bulletin board dotted with tacked-on coupons.

Another important trick is to buy large quantities of sale items for which you have coupons. Recently, a market at which I shop advertised White Cloud toilet paper for 77 cents per four-roll package. I had saved eight coupons good for 25 cents off each purchase of two four-roll packages. Since the market doubles coupons, this meant that I could buy each package for 52 cents. I bought sixteen packages, storing them in the basement. The following week, the store returned to the normal price of $1.29. I saved $12.32 (77 cents on each of the sixteen packages) on the sort of humdrum product that I hate to spend money on.

These sorts of triple plays (sale prices matched with coupons that are then doubled) are commonplace for well-organized shoppers. On another trip, my store advertised Bounty paper towels for 59 cents and 8-ounce bottles of Seven Seas salad dressing also for 59 cents. Each of the products is usually $1.09. I had twelve 10-cent coupons for the paper towels; doubled, I paid 39 cents for each roll. I had six 50-cent coupons for the salad dressing; the store doubled these to the purchase price (59 cents), so I got the six bottles free. So, for items costing normal shoppers $19.62, I paid $4.68, a savings of 76 percent. And, I got *good* products. Name-brand paper towels really are thicker, stronger, and more absorbent than discount brands. And as for discount salad dressings, well, I'm a little leery about putting into my family's bodies food that some manufacturer has cut corners on. So I seek and create opportunities to get name-brand products at discount-brand prices. Of course there are no opportunities to be seen, or taken, if you haven't prepared for them. That preparation is accomplished through Step Two of the Super Coupon Shopping System, summarized in the points on the following page.

Step-Two Summary

1. **Collect coupons.** Remember that there are hundreds of billions of dollars in coupons circulating. They are available to anyone who is alert to them and willing to gather them. Make use of the five sources of coupons.

2. **Organize your coupons.** Create a simple, portable system in which you can easily file and find your coupons. Be attentive to expiration dates. Put thought into creating your coupon categories. Remember, most people wind up living permanently with their initial systems, no matter how arbitrary filing later becomes.

3. **Multiply the value of your coupons.** Use coupons in combination with store sales, store coupons, and double-coupon promotions at stores.

4. **Shop to your advantage.** Buy name brands because you are most likely to find manufacturer discounts for these products. Don't, however, be loyal to particular brands; buy products that provide the best value at the time you shop. Buy small sizes, increasing coupon values, and buy large numbers of high-value items.

5. **Organize your trip at home.** Prepare an informative and well-structured shopping list. The list should indicate items that you expect to realize savings on and items for which you have coupons. Arrange it, if possible, in the same order in which products are found in the store.

6. **Bring all your coupons to the store.** If you use my method, during your trip you'll separate from your main file the coupons you will use. Even if you separate those coupons into a different envelope before you shop, you should bring the rest of your coupons to take advantage of unadvertised specials and trial sizes.

· STEP THREE ·

Refunding: Money from Shopping

--- ✂

It is certainly nice enough to watch the stunned expressions on other shoppers' faces when my grocery bill is reduced by half or more by the stack of coupons presented to the cashier. Even nicer, though, is the somewhat more private pleasure gained from monthly deposits of $100 to $150 received from manufacturers who are literally paying me to use their products.

Every month for the last twenty years I've received about 200 pieces of mail from some of America's largest corporations. Every one of those pieces has contained something of value for me. As one talk show host noted, "I bet you love for the postman to come, right? He's bringing you money."

Well, the mail carrier is bringing me more than just money. There are three kinds of bounty that these manufacturers send me. The first is the nicest, money in the form of either cash or checks. The second kind is coupons, usually good for receiving products absolutely free. And third, I get gifts, what manufacturers call premiums. All these I receive for buying products, cutting out and saving scraps of paper, and filling out forms. The whole process is what is known as refunding.

Refunding, as with couponing, requires an initial time

51

investment and then a regular commitment of one to three hours per week. Refunds (or rebates, as many refunders call them) lie at the heart of the Super Coupon Shopper System. With refunds I've not only created that $35,000 college fund mentioned in the Introduction, but I've also received the "free product" coupons responsible for my most successful shopping outings, and I've received hundreds of useful gifts, ranging from toys through clothing to small appliances. The time investment certainly pays handsome rewards.

Refunding Explained

Refunds are essentially rewards given by manufacturers to consumers who use their products. Manufacturers offer refunds for essentially the same reasons they provide coupons. They wish to introduce shoppers to new products, to promote improvements in existing products, or to lure consumers away from their competitors' products.

Refund offers are different from coupons in four critical respects.

First, coupon savings are realized immediately. You get to watch the glorious list of price reductions roll across the cash register window. Refunds appear in the forms of checks or cash some weeks after you've sent in for them.

Second, while coupons always take the form of some sort of cash savings off a grocery bill, refunds can take one of three forms. They will be either a direct cash or check rebate on a purchase, a coupon to be used on a future purchase, or some type of merchandise delivered to your door.

Third, while coupon savings are accomplished merely with the production of the coupon for the purchased product, refunds usually require that *proofs of purchase* be mailed to the company. Usually an entry blank called a *refund form* (or *required blank*) must also be included, accompanied by the *cash register tape* showing that the required product was purchased.

The fourth difference is the one that provides the great benefits of refunding, benefits that more than balance the nuisances apparent in the first three differences. While the average value of coupons is about 50 cents, the cash value of refunds is almost always at least twice that, routinely in the two- to five-dollar range, and can easily reach $15. In fact, some refunding values are truly staggering. Just two years ago, the purchase of two simple Procter & Gamble products (such as a shampoo and a deodorant) garnered four travel certificates worth $85 each off the price of American Airlines airfares. That's a potential savings of $340 through the purchase of products costing about 1 percent of the final rebate. Refunding may take a little more time than coupon clipping, but it pays off.

The Process

An elaborate industry has grown up around the simple one- and two-dollar rebate checks that are the hallmark of the refunding system. The mechanics by which this process operates are, however, quite simple.

First, the manufacturer offers a refund to all customers who purchase a specified product. The offer may take any of three shapes:

• A readily available form is distributed to consumers, describing the offer and the qualifications needed to comply with the offer.

• Offers are made that require the consumer to write

directly to the manufacturer to receive the forms necessary for compliance with the offer.

• Offers are made requiring no forms; the consumer merely sends in the necessary qualifying materials and a note identifying the offer.

Excedrin, for example, recently offered a $2 refund on some of its products, advertising the refund in stores, with pads containing the necessary forms attached to the shelves next to the products. (I know, the process of controlling all the materials needed to refund successfully makes the use of an Excedrin example seem particularly apt; trust me when I tell you that refunding is not an Excedrin headache but an Excedrin—and other manufacturers'—reward).

Next, the refunder takes one of the forms, fills it out, and mails it to the address given, along with whatever proofs of purchase are required. In this case, Excedrin required the entire, flattened, carton that had contained the bottle of tablets and a cash register tape with the product price circled.

Then, the form and its proofs of purchase arrive at their destination, usually not the manufacturer, but an organization known as a redemption agency or clearinghouse. These agencies process hundreds of different refund offers for hundreds of different manufacturers. They are, for the most part, completely independent of the manufacturers and thus are ineffective in dealing with consumer complaints. Some of the most common clearinghouses have P.O. Box addresses in the cities of Clinton, Iowa; Douglas and Sierra Vista, Arizona; El Paso, Texas; and Young America, Minnesota.

Finally, the clearinghouse processes the refund request, determining that all the necessary *qualifiers*, or proofs of purchase, have been sent. In the Excedrin example, having verified receipt of the flattened box and cash register tape, the agency would then mail out a check for $2. The process, from mailing of qualifiers to receipt of check, usually takes from four to eight weeks, with the range running from two to twelve weeks.

That, simply, is the process. A product is purchased, the packaging is saved and sent to the manufacturer's representative, who then sends the purchaser money. It's the best recycling program I know of.

Falling Through the Cracks

Refunding is a practice most shoppers ignore, an ignorance that is expensive and unnecessary. Super Shoppers, however, use refunding effectively, not just for its own benefits, but because it interfaces so well with couponing. As we'll see, expert couponers are the people most able to become expert refunders. It's an achievement that can be reached at relatively slight cost and with pretty decent benefits.

Recall my purchase of sixteen packages of White Cloud discussed in the previous chapter. I used a shopping triple play there, combining a store sale with my coupons, which were then doubled by the store, to save $12.32. Well, the wrappers from those sixteen packages will be used to gain a refunding triple play. I'll save certain parts of those wrappers because I know that there will be a White Cloud refund offer worth one or two dollars at some point in the future.

I'm pretty certain of this because I've been refunding for a while now, and I know that the parent corporation of White Cloud, Procter & Gamble, is the company that offers more refunds than any other. When they offer a White Cloud refund, I'll be ready, and I'll achieve yet

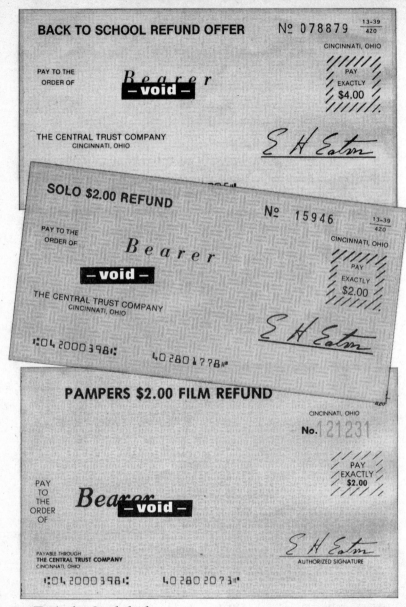

Typical refund checks

more savings on the product. It'll be my second triple play: store savings combined with coupon savings combined with the company's money-back refund offer.

In fact, these refunding triple plays have resulted in my *never*, in the last ten years, paying even a nickel for certain products for which I know I can always, with patience, find a combined promotion. Some of these products are spaghetti sauce, toilet paper, facial tissues, paper towels, and various kinds of candy. For ten years, my family of six has spent nothing on these products, nothing.

I don't think most shoppers like paying for all these products, yet, oddly, most do. Few people utilize the benefits of refunding for, I think, three reasons.

The first is that people are just unaware of the opportunities awaiting them. Refund offers are rarely distributed as aggressively as coupons. Most are either hidden in the service departments of the stores, lost in the clutter of the store's shelving, obscured by all the other information on a product's package, or publicized only among the diligent. The System will make you one of the privileged who knows where to look and how to find this gold mine of offers.

The second problem is that people know of refunding but are sure that refunders, to amass the qualifying package parts required by manufacturers, must deal with an unorganizable, jumbled litter of labels, boxes, and bottles. With the right system, though, anything is organizable. And the Super Coupon Shopper System has gone through twenty years of practice to get it right.

Finally, some people are certain that anything that provides this sort of steady income must require all sorts of tax reporting to be legal. Well, they're wrong. Refund money is tax-free. The IRS considers all refunds to be not taxable income but simply reductions in the purchase price of items already purchased. Since you already pay income tax on the money used to purchase those items, and you already paid any sales taxes at the time of purchase, you don't have to pay any more taxes on that money. Even the IRS won't tax the same money twice.

Three Easy Steps: The Refunder's SOS

Entering the refunding society can be overwhelming at first. There's a mass of qualifying material to sift through, decisions to be made about what to save, and then the problem of organizing it all into some coherent, usable form. Even finding out about offers often seems to rely more on voodoo than on skill. The novice feels like she should be sending out a constant Mayday signal.

There really is no crisis, however, that can't be handled by the self-reliant principles of the refunder's SOS:

• Save everything that might be useful and helpful.
• Organize your materials, time, and labor efficiently.
• Send for money, for forms, and for information on a regular and consistent basis.

There are two basic approaches to refunding, one requiring more effort and one offering fewer rewards but taking less time. In selecting the approach most useful to you, consider how much time you want to spend on the exercise and to what degree the time spent will seem rewarding, both in financial savings and by engaging in the activity itself.

Saving

The Comprehensive Method: Save Everything

The refunder who wants to get everything has to save just about everything. For whatever reason (and at times while

I'm struggling to soak off labels or slice parts of plastic bottles, those reasons appear to have decidedly perverse origins), manufacturers will choose from any of a variety of package parts to request as qualifiers for their refund offers.

Typical proof of purchase seals

The two most common parts requested are proof of purchase seals (POPs) and universal product code seals (UPCs).

POPs are sections of packages containing the legend "proof of purchase" or some similar phrase like "purchase confirmation" or "purchase seal." They are usually enclosed within a dotted or bold line and are often found on the inner flaps of packages. Increasingly, products are being found with the POP legend written above the UPC. Not all products contain specifically labeled POPs.

UPCs are found on just about every product. These are the piano-keyboard-like symbols with numbers written below them that are scanned at the checkout counter.

Although POPs and UPCs are the qualifiers most often requested, unfortunately there are numerous others used by manufacturers.

Some of the more common are net weight statements, size designations, product names, box tops or bottoms, ingredient panels, tear strips, labels, and cap liners. Unfortunately, manufacturers change their requirements. Pampers, for example, after years of requiring the use of the size designation suddenly began requesting the

UPC seals

words "Disposable Diapers."

So, if you can't know which part of a package a manufacturer is going to request—and you can't—and you want to profit from every offer made, then your only recourse is to save basically everything. For those going this route, I've prepared the following list of what needs to be saved:

Batteries: Entire cardboard backing.

Bottles: Front, back, and neck label; cap liner.

Bread and Bagel Wrappers: All parts that contain printing.

Bulbs: Entire outer wrapper, flattened.

Butter, Margarine, Cream Cheese: Entire outer box.

Cake Mixes and Frostings: Can labels, box tops and bottoms, net weight statements.

Candy: Entire outer wrapper.

Cans and Jars: Entire label.

Cereals, Cookies, Crackers: Box top, bottom, and POP, usually on side of box or on inside flap.

Cigarettes: Entire individual packages (remove cellophane and foil), carton end flaps.

Cleaners: Net weight and opening paper tab.

Coffee: Label and inner seal from instant; plastic lid and label from ground.

Dog and Cat Food: POPs, weight circles, entire outer wraps from bagged food.

Frozen Foods: Entire outer cartons, peeling away thicker backing if possible.

Gravy and Salad Dressing Mixes: Entire envelope.

Health and Beauty Aids: Entire box; individual Band-Aid and Steri-pad wrappers, toothpaste boxes, razor and blade cardboard backings; basically any printed cardboard parts and paper.

Juice: Opening strip from frozen cans; words "fresh if used by above date" from Minute Maid.

Paper Napkins, Toilet Paper, Paper Towels: Entire plastic overwrap that contains printing.

Plastic Bottles: Front and back labels; snap lids on shampoo.

Potato and Corn Chips, Pretzels, etc.: Complete wrapper.

Small Appliances: Warranty card, owner's manual, sales slip.

Sneakers: Code number from box and sales slip.

Soda: Cap liners, labels, and neck bands from bottles; imprints from plastic carriers; POPs from cardboard carriers.

Sugar, Rice, and Flour: Entire paper package; box bottoms, net weights, and POPs.

Tea: Entire front panel showing net weight from boxes; inner seal and front label from instant.

Tissues: Opening tear strip; UPC; quality seal.

Toys: Product number from box, instruction manual or back card, sales slip.

Underwear: Entire package and sales slip.

Generally save all UPCs and anything with a POP-type label.

Of course, whatever you've decided to not save, because it wasn't on this list, will somehow turn up in an offer. The only alternative is to truly save everything, which can create pretty significant household strains.

A quick reading of the list shows that some of these qualifiers are things not easily removed from their packages, while others appear to be quite bulky. Over the years, refunders have come up with innovative ways of dealing with these problems.

The most difficult qualifiers to remove are labels that

Typical free-product coupons

have been glued on to plastic bottles. Here are some solutions suggested by experienced refunders:

• Get double use out of your washer and dryer. Fill bottles and jars with water and let them lie in the stationary tub on wash day. Waste water from the washer will cover and loosen the labels. Peel them and place on a sheet of newspaper, paste side up, on top of the dryer, whose heat then dries the labels.

• Fill empty plastic bottles with very hot water and let them sit for about two minutes. Peel the labels and let them dry (they're sticky) on a paper towel.

• Place a wadded, soaked paper towel directly over the label and seal the container in a plastic bag. Let it sit for at least two hours and the label will slip off.

• Soak the labels for about five minutes in hot water and dish soap.

• Hold the container under warm water and gently ease the label off using a single-edge razor blade or X-acto knife.

• Dry soaked labels by sticking them, glue-side out, against the side of the refrigerator.

• Remove labels from products used around water (like dish detergent) before they are used, as labels are more difficult to remove if they've gotten wet and then dried on the container.

• Steam labels off by using a steam iron or holding over a kettle.

The glue used on these labels is tenacious. Always place the removed labels paste side up when drying, or be prepared to soak them off again.

Cans and glass jars have labels that are usually attached by only one strip of glue. Such labels can be easily removed by slitting them down one side, away from the glued strip.

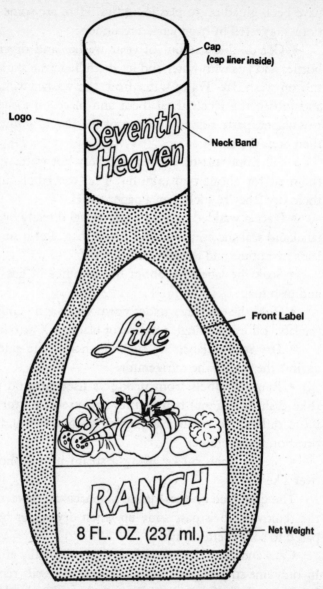

A bottle (front) with potential qualifiers labeled by part

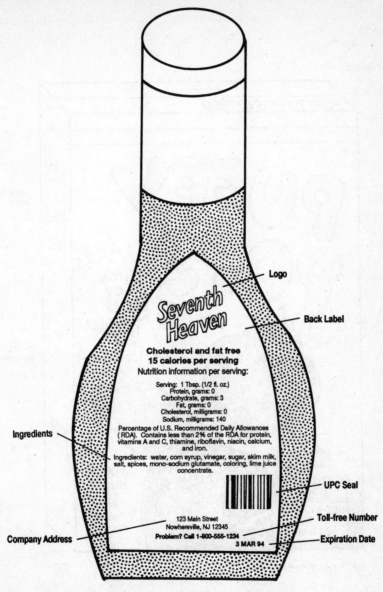

Logo

Seventh Heaven

Back Label

Cholesterol and fat free
15 calories per serving
Nutrition information per serving:

Serving: 1 Tbsp. (1/2 fl. oz.)
Protein, grams: 0
Carbohydrate, grams: 3
Fat, grams: 0
Cholesterol, milligrams: 0
Sodium, milligrams: 140

Percentage of U.S. Recommended Daily Allowances
(RDA). Contains less than 2% of the RDA for protein,
vitamins A and C, thiamine, riboflavin, niacin, calcium,
and iron.

Ingredients

Ingredients: water, corn syrup, vinegar, sugar, skim milk,
salt, spices, mono-sodium glutamate, coloring, lime juice
concentrate.

UPC Seal

123 Main Street
Nowhereville, NJ 12345
Company Address
Problem? Call 1-800-555-1234

Toll-free Number

3 MAR 94   **Expiration Date**

A bottle (back) with potential qualifiers labeled by part

A box with potential qualifiers labeled by part

Box qualifiers are easy to remove, but the bulky size of the cardboard leads many refunders to seek ways to minimize that size. Some people try to peel off the layer of the box containing all the printing. Two methods are to use either some form of sharp edge, such as a razor, or even a fingernail, or to moisten the boxes and let them sit in a sealed plastic bag overnight, making the printed layer easy to peel off. Finally, flatten the parts that are being saved.

Minimize the bulk of plastic wrappings from paper goods and breads by cutting off the end parts, which contain no printing.

Qualifiers: The Easy Way

Now, I know that to many people all this qualifier collecting sounds like exactly the kind of trouble that's kept them away from refunding. For many others, it is as much a hobby (and as valid a one, I think, as collecting things like stamps or baseball cards) as a method of saving large sums of money. For those less inclined to make this kind of time expenditure, there's an easier, and still quite remunerative, method.

Simply save only POPs, UPCs, and net weight statements. About 80 percent of all refund offers rely on these fairly easy to collect seals. I confess that after years of collecting everything, I now save primarily these. As a result, I do miss out on some offers, but for now the time investment for complete qualifier collecting would be too burdensome for me and would make this all more like work than fun.

Many UPCs and POPs now are labeled by the manufacturer with the product name and, sometimes, size. If this information is not on the POP or UPC, you must write it on the back or you'll have numerous scraps of useless cardboard. Manufacturers want only *their* qualifiers sent in, and they know, from the information imbedded in the UPC, the type and size of the product from which that UPC seal came. If it isn't the UPC symbol from the proper product, they'll refuse your refund request.

Because many refunders are unfortunate enough to have a number of these orphan UPCs, I've listed in Appendix D some common product UPCs. These indicate brand names, but not sizes. Nevertheless, you'll be able to use the brand codes to generally identify your UPCs, which can then be more specifically matched with size and brand UPCs at the market.

The Additional Qualifier: Cash Register Tapes

The other thing all refunders must save are cash register tapes (CRTs). Increasing numbers of offers require that qualifiers be matched with tapes showing that the products were actually purchased. The most obvious problem with using these CRTs is dealing with the dilemma of responding to multiple refund offers for products that were purchased in the same shopping trip and therefore share the same CRT. The problem has two pretty simple solutions.

The easiest is to cut up the CRT and send the appropriate portion to each offer being responded to. I've done this for years, and I've never been refused my refund. In fact, I've never heard of any refunder being refused for sending in a partial CRT. When using these, it is wise to write the store name and date on the CRT, especially if the offer requests such information.

The alternative solution is to request from the store a "rebate receipt" when you know that you've purchased multiple rebate items. These are forms with spaces to be

Store refund coupons

filled in by the store showing that specified products were purchased at the store for a certain price on a certain date. I've also never been refused one of these forms.

Finding the Offers

Saving all these qualifiers and CRTs is a pretty forlorn exercise if you don't have a place to send them. There are six principal sources of information about refund offers:

1. The stores. Store forms on tear-off pads can usually be found in any of three places: near the customer-service counter, on bulletin boards near the entrance, and mounted on the shelves or as part of special displays alongside the products. Customers are expected to tear off only the one form they are permitted to use. Unfortunately, some people take large numbers of forms so that they can sell the forms to other refunders. This makes store forms somewhat difficult to come by. The best chances for acquiring these forms are midweek, Tuesday through Thursday, when the manufacturers' representatives who distribute these forms are most likely to be restocking store shelves. Even when all the forms have been taken, it is still possible to learn of refund offers through information printed on the cardboard backing upon which the forms were attached.

These *cardboard backings* provide two different types of relief for refunders lacking forms. One instructs the refunder to send the necessary qualifiers to a given address in order to receive the refund. The other kind requests the refunder to send a request to a specific address for the necessary form. Once the form is received, the refunder fills it out and mails

Typical cardboard backing

it along with the relevant qualifiers for the refund.

Cardboard backings are obviously important to refunders. Where cardboard backings are the only remnant of a refund offer, considerate refunders jot down the relevant information and leave the backing in place for others to use.

Another type of in-store form appears on the products themselves. These are called *hang tags* and, sadly, tend to disappear more rapidly than do the products upon which they are hung.

A third in-store form is printed directly on a package or placed inside a box. These are called "specially marked packages" or SMPs in refunders' jargon. They are most

Typical hang tags

Typical magazine form

prevalent among health and beauty aids, cereals, pet products, and detergents.

2. Newspapers and magazines. These often contain forms not only for cash refunds but also for receiving coupons for free samples of products. The best sources for these are the same as those for coupons. Watch the "food day" in your local newspaper, the free-standing inserts, and the various "women's" magazines.

3. Home mailers. Refund offers often appear alongside the coupons distributed by these mailing services. Active refunders find themselves quickly appearing on various mailing lists and tend to receive a fairly large number of unsolicited offers in the mail. Refunders hoping to increase the volume of mail received can write to the following addresses:

Donnelly Marketing, 1235 N. Avenue, Nevada,

IA 50201, distributes the Carol Wright mailers, which are sent out several times a year.

Direct Marketing Association, 6 East 43rd Street, New York, NY 10017, acts as an umbrella for numerous marketers. Correspondence must specify the desire to receive either more or less direct mail.

4. The manufacturers. As was discussed above, it is often necessary to request refund forms from manufacturers when store supplies have been exhausted. There are also times when you learn from a friend or through the grapevine that an offer is available for which you have neither forms nor cardboard-backing information. In such circumstances, you can write directly to the consumer-relations department of the company. All the major firms now have such departments, and a few are quite helpful in supplying missing forms. Appendix C contains a list of company addresses.

5. Refunding newsletters. These newsletters provide refunders with two important services. Refunders are given up-to-date information about which refund offers are available, and they are given the opportunity to trade forms and qualifiers with other refunders.

There is probably no better way to gain information about refunds than by subscribing to a newsletter. Subscribers to these bulletins are also participants, providing information about current refunds in each issue. Each subscriber gets hooked into a network of eyes and ears, all searching for the common objective: bargains. Subscribers also benefit from a national circulation by being able to learn of refund offers that are publicized only in some regions, although they are redeemable nationally.

There are currently about ten such newsletters in the country. I'm quite partial to my own, *Refundle Bundle*, P. O.

Box 140, Centuck Station, Yonkers, NY 10710, which I'll discuss in some detail in the next chapter. Three others are: *Moneytalk*, Larksville, PA; *Refund Express*, Monroe, GA; and *D & J's Refund Reporter*, Corpus Christi, TX.

6. Clubs and conventions. As noted above regarding the newsletters, refunding succeeds best when people can share information. Two ways they do this are through local clubs and regional conventions. Information about both can be obtained through newsletters and by scanning the community bulletin boards in local supermarkets. Two sources of convention information are: Gloria Murphy, Route 2, Box 153, Jefferson, IA 50129; and Wendy Miller, 246 E. Rice, Owatonna, MN 55060. Enclose a self-addresed, stamped return envelope with your request.

Organize Everything

Qualifiers add up to a lot of paper very quickly. It's paper that, just as with coupons, needs to be brought under control if effective use is to be made of it. Unfortunately, the shape, size, and labeling (or as common with UPCs, the *lack* of labeling) of qualifiers make their organization especially daunting. But it can be done; in fact if it isn't done, you might find your living space overrun by packaging.

Organizing a comprehensive collection of qualifiers looks close to impossible, but anyone with the fortitude to remove and collect all these qualifiers can certainly organize them. All refunders, by nature, approach their collections with two similar goals. First, since the qualifiers are kept only for the purpose of bringing in checks, which they can't do if they can't be located, there has to be some way of gaining access to the ones you want. Second, whatever method is used to organize these things so that they can be accessed should be inexpensive, or else the whole point of the process is lost.

The system I used when I collected everything succeeded in these goals and typifies the systems used by comprehensive refunders. My organizing materials consisted of a plastic produce bag, a few shoe boxes, and one large envelope.

The plastic bag was kept in a kitchen drawer. I would put into it my qualifiers as I detached them from the packages. I've always found it easiest to remove the qualifiers as I finish the product rather than letting packages accumulate. Once the bag was filled, usually in about three to four weeks, I'd haul it over to my shoe boxes.

I had six boxes, ranging in size from 3"x 3"x 5"to 24"x 18"x 10". All were kept in the garage in a space of about 2' x 2', not much more floor space than that taken up by a kitchen chair. In these boxes I arranged my qualifiers by size and product name.

In the small box I kept, divided by manila envelopes, POPs cut out of boxes and bags. In the shoe boxes were kept small labels; in boot boxes I kept the larger labels, and in the largest box I kept flattened boxes, plastic wrappings, and large labels. In each box, all the qualifiers were alphabetized by product name.

That was it: a plastic bag I got free from the market, some old shoe and boot boxes, and a cardboard carton. Hardly elaborate, but the source of thousands of dollars in cash, hundreds of useful gifts, and thousands of coupons.

Most serious refunders have similar systems. Few are willing to give up house space to packaging parts, so they create ingenious storage methods. One woman keeps all her qualifiers—nearly thirty cartons full—on a roll-out platform beneath her bed.

Organizing Qualifiers: The Minimalist Collection

Not surprisingly, it's much easier to organize qualifiers when they are limited to net weight statements, POPs, and UPCs. The system is similar to that for the comprehensive collection of qualifiers, but certainly simpler.

I remove qualifiers from packages as I finish the product. I write on the back of the qualifiers size and product-name information if it is not already on them. The qualifiers are stashed in an envelope in my kitchen drawer until there's a large enough number to warrant filing. Then they are filed in a small box that is divided by manila envelopes and arranged alphabetically by product name. My qualifiers now take up not much more space than do my coupon files.

Organizing Cash Register Tapes

Cash register tapes are definitely a hassle to deal with. Unfortunately, offers requiring CRTs are no longer the rare exception—now roughly a third to half of all refund offers include the request for CRTC (cash register tape circled) to be mailed with the qualifiers.

The problems with CRTs are that each contains information needed for numerous different offers and, on many CRTs, that information is not very clearly labeled. There are two approaches for dealing with CRTs, each with its usefulness determined by the amount of information included on the CRT.

The simplest method is the least organized. Just keep all CRTs in one envelope and go through it as you need a CRT proof to complete a refund offer. This process creates obvious difficulties in that most CRTs do not include specific product names near the prices. I've found that educated guessing works quite well in these situations. I just find a CRT with a

Rebate receipt, normal CRT, and itemized CRT

price that seems to fit my recollection of the price that I paid
for the product. I then send in this CRT (or part of the CRT,
if I might need the rest for other products). I have never
been refused for using CRTs this way, and I believe that I am
complying with the integrity of the rebate offers because I
have purchased the products and I am making good-faith
efforts to find the exact CRTs that prove those purchases.
And if I get truly stumped about the purchase price of a
product in my attempt to find the right CRT, I can always
get pricing information from the store. This process of scanning CRTs is not difficult if you do three things:

1. Save all your CRTs.

2. Look through CRTs only for products you have
   purchased.

3. Know the approximate price of the product for
   which you need the CRT.

It rarely takes me more than a minute to go through

my CRTs to find what I need to complete the offers requiring them.

The other method is more difficult and time consuming. When unpacking your groceries, note on your CRT, near the relevant prices, products you've purchased for which refund offers are possible. Then either cut up the CRT and file the pieces along with the relevant qualifiers, or just keep the CRTs all piled together and review them as needed for use. Some stores make the cut-up-and-file method easier by including on the CRTs exact product-name information for everything purchased.

A third method for dealing with CRTs is to file the necessary parts of them with any rebate forms that state the need for CRTs. This, of course, works only for offers about which you are aware before shopping.

Another trick, where you know that you will need CRTs to complete an offer, is to get rebate receipts from the store. These, as I mentioned earlier, are issued by the stores upon consumer request, individually for particular products, showing that the product was purchased at the store. They are usually issued at the customer-service desk. Once received, they can then be kept clipped to the rebate offers for which they will be used.

Generally, CRTs can be some trouble, but with experience and patience, they can be handled effectively.

Organizing the Refund Forms

All this cutting, sorting, and filing of qualifiers is useless if you can't send them out to meet manufacturers' requests. The basis of being able to meet deadlines and fulfill qualifier requirements lies in keeping a well-organized file of rebate forms.

I keep all my forms in one large envelope, similar to the envelope I use for storing my cash-offs. The forms are filed alphabetically by product, with expiration dates circled. I monitor these forms pretty closely; too much trouble goes into assembling qualifiers for me to miss an offer because I've overlooked an expiration date.

I pull those forms for which I expect to meet all qualifications when they near their expiration dates and paper clip to them the qualifiers I already have on hand. I keep these in kitchen drawers and add new qualifiers as I obtain them.

Another method used by some refunders to avoid missing expiration dates is to keep a small notebook in which they enter the offers due to expire at the end of the month and the number of qualifiers needed to fulfill the offer's terms. Then, as they shop during the month, they can buy those products necessary to gain the qualifiers, providing, of course, that they want the products and can gain Super Shopper savings on them.

Send, Send, Send

The mail carrier, if not the refunder's best friend is certainly one of her most important allies. Not only does the mail bring money, coupons, and gifts, but it is also the vehicle by which the process is initiated. Refunders send out three things through the mail:

1. Completed forms and qualifiers that bring them their rebates.
2. Requests for forms.
3. Requests for information.

The most time-consuming of these is the first, mailing out to the companies all the required forms and qualifiers necessary to receive the rebates. It is also the part of the process that *costs* money. I, of course, try to keep both of these costs down.

A diligent refunder will also need to send out two types of requests. From manufacturers, refunders can request forms and information about forms, as when they come across cardboard backings from which all the forms have been removed. The other type of request will be covered thoroughly in the next chapter. The requests of this type are primarily of other refunders, all of whom are linked in a sort of underground network. Through this network, refunders share information about offers, about manufacturer compliance, and about trades with one another of forms and qualifiers. It is a vital part of the refunding process, and one not at all difficult to become a part of.

Rebating is like every other form of correspondence— you only receive mail regularly if you also send it out regularly. To gain my monthly $100 to $150, I have to send out about 100 pieces of mail each month. That's a lot of envelopes to address. The burden is lessened by spacing out the addressing throughout the month. Generally, I try to address while I'm doing something else, like watching TV, doing the laundry, or idly chatting with someone. My folder of "envelopes to be addressed"is sort of a refunder's knitting basket, a little chore that occupies my hands while my mind is more engaged on something else.

Expediting the Process

There are a few tricks to expedite this process. One is to reduce the time spent filling in your return address on the envelopes. The easiest method for dealing with this is to get a self-inking stamp printed up (they usually cost under ten dollars) and use it. You can also order return-address labels to stick on to the envelopes. I believe, though, that the stamp works out to be cheaper and requires less time to use than the labels.

One other simple method: Abbreviate wherever possible. Most obviously, do this by abbreviating the names of the states to which the refund offers are being sent. Appendix E is a list of the authorized abbreviations issued by the United States Postal Service.

Another method is to reduce the time spent on actual addressing by relying on a personal computer with a printer that can print out labels. As most refund offers are sent to one of the major clearinghouses, it would be possible to print out large numbers of labels containing spaces for the name of the rebate offer (if required), the P.O. Box number, and the last four digits of a nine-digit zip code. The labels could be preprinted with cities, states, and five-digit codes. Appendix F contains a list of major clearinghouse city, state, and zip code addresses. If considering this method, of course, one has to weigh the cost of the labels against the time savings, remembering that the primary purpose of all this is to save money. The financial savings, though, shouldn't come at the cost of turning this into a burden.

However you address the envelopes, you don't want any of the addressing to be in vain. The one piece of mail refunders don't appreciate is the one containing a note that begins "We regret to inform you..." To avoid these refusals, keep the following points in mind:

• Send the proper qualifiers. You must send exactly the parts of the packaging requested *and* you must send those

Various Procter & Gamble qualifiers

parts from the exact size and type of product requested. A refund offer requiring proofs from two 32-ounce bottles of Era detergent will not accept proofs from one or even two 64-ounce bottles. An offer requesting proofs from four regular cans of Campbell's soups will not accept labels from the more expensive Campbell's Healthy Choice soups. Always send in *exactly* what the offer calls for.

• Check the expiration date of the form. As with cash-offs, many rebate offers are marked with EDs. These can take two forms:

—The most common simply notes that the offer expires on a specified date. These EDs require that the refund request be postmarked by that date.

—The other type, usually appearing only along with the first type, requires that products be purchased within a certain time frame and requires a dated CRT as proof to be submitted with the qualifiers.

It is a good idea to highlight these dates on your forms so that you stay aware of them. Occasionally, companies extend their offers, especially when a form is requested from them close to the time it will expire. You can't, however, expect regular grants of this form of largesse. It's best to make a strong effort to meet all deadlines.

• Be patient. Although most refunds are received within six weeks of the request, they can take longer.

—Don't contact the company until twelve weeks have lapsed. Once in a while, a company has trouble filling their requests, but these problems rarely extend beyond three months.

—Contact the company, not the clearinghouse. It is a complete waste of time to contact the address to which the refund request has been sent. Whenever you have trouble with a rebate, contact the consumer-relations department of the company offering the rebate. A list of company addresses is contained in Appendix D. Also, many companies now have toll-free phone numbers to handle customer complaints. These numbers can be found on product packages and at local libraries in the *Consumers' Directory of 800 Telephone Numbers.*

Bending the Rules

It is important to avoid being too rigid in applying any of the principles of the System. Especially when dealing with refunding, it's important to remember that manufacturers offer these programs largely for the purpose of building goodwill among consumers. Sometimes, their rules, such as expiration dates on offers, can be bent. When a particularly good value is available, a late request may be worth the investment of postage costs.

An example is provided by the experience of one refunder in Texas. On a day that she had purchased two pairs of Haggar slacks she also bought a six-pack of Star-Kist tuna fish that contained a $2-rebate form on the Haggar slacks. Noticing, though, that the rebate form had expired two months earlier, she nevertheless mailed it to Haggar with a note explaining her late receipt of the form and requesting that Haggar relax its rule on the expiration date. The company responded, stating their inability to extend the rebate program but offering her another, free pair of their slacks. She called the 800 number they provided and received a pair of slacks in the size, color, and material she requested. She later went to a store and discovered that the slacks sent her were retailing for $23.

Obviously, not all such stories are so happily resolved, because manufacturers don't want their EDs to become superfluous messages on the forms, but it is not uncommon for manufacturers to offer refunders some compensation for requesting rebates on expired offers. Generally, a refunder's best chance of gaining this type of corporate generosity occurs when, as with the Haggar example, the rebate offer is processed directly by the company rather than by one of the clearinghouses.

Postage and Supplies

Finally, there's the financial cost of refunding: buying stamps and envelopes. There is little that can be done about the purchase of postage. The post office has yet to issue coupons or refund certificates, and we're pretty much stuck with using first class postage. Regulations governing the use of third class mail are strict and require that a fairly large number of identically sized pieces be sent to each individual zip code. It is possible for groups of refunders to pool their mailings every month to take advantage of this rate. Complete details of third class rules are available at local post offices.

Envelopes are a different story. Buy them cheaply and often. I look for clearance sales, especially sidewalk sales where groups of merchants clear out products that aren't selling. Stationers at these events often sell large bundles of oddly shaped and colored envelopes at very low prices. Besides meeting the Super Shopper test of being cheap, mailing out refunds in these envelopes adds a bit of frivolity to the process. One of the more ingenious methods of acquiring envelopes, suggested by a longtime refunder, is to seek from local printers envelopes that have been misprinted. The refunder marks out or covers with his own label the printed return address. The person who suggested this gets her envelopes as cheaply as $4 per thousand. So, where there's a will, there's a way, and where there's a Super Shopper, there's a cheaper way.

Keeping Records

Although recordkeeping is not a necessary function of refunding, many refunders keep some form of log for a number of reasons.

Logs help us gain maximum control of the refunding process. Logs containing information about form expiration dates and qualifiers on hand enhance the ability of refunders to meet rebate deadlines. And because a missed deadline is money that will never find its way into your pocket, a useful log can make the difference between refunding simply for the pleasure of collecting and refunding for pleasure and profit.

Logs keep us from sending out requests that won't be fulfilled. Since most refund offers limit the number of rebates each family may receive, refunders record the offers that they have already sent for to avoid repeating a request that would then be denied by the company.

Refunders like to track company response to refund requests. Most importantly, they want to know the causes of any delay in receiving their rebates. Keeping a record showing when forms and qualifiers were sent allows refunders to follow up their requests in the rare instances when a company either has not complied with or has refused to honor a rebate request within twelve or so weeks of the request's mailing.

Rebaters like to know how well they've done. Many keep logs showing the money returned to them and the gifts sent by manufacturers. They're not necessary, but it can be personally gratifying to see exactly how much all those one- to five-dollar checks add up to each month. And, the logs provide evidence for the bragging about our shopping savvy we all like to engage in, at least occasionally.

Logs also help us in making decisions about which qualifiers to keep. In the hope that history has *some* utility, we may decide to save, for future use, those qualifiers that particular manufacturers have requested in the past. Our individual logs are the only sources of that information.

For rebaters interested in keeping a log of this sort, page 146 contains a sample Rebate Log Form that can be copied and used for recordkeeping.

Another method of recordkeeping is to use the appliance that seems likely to dominate the new century into which we are rushing: the personal computer. For those rebaters in possession of one of these machines and, unlike me, in possession of the skills with which to use it, refunding software is being marketed.

One such program, entitled the "Shopper's Helper," is offered by Cosmos Software. It permits the shopper to maintain records of all qualifiers and forms on hand along with information about offers that have been sent away for. The program also permits shoppers to keep records of their coupons, tracking products, brand names, value, and EDs.

Using either the coupon or refunding functions of the program is accomplished fairly simply by selecting products and brands from lists stored in the program and then entering specific information about value, EDs, and qualifiers. Although shoppers will still need to search through their coupon and qualifier inventories to use cash-offs and refund offers, this type of program creates a way of knowing whether or not the search would be futile or fruitful.

The "Shopper's Helper" program is available for a free 30-day trial from Cosmos Software, 29735 Nova Woods Drive, Farmington Hills, MI 48331-1996.

This chapter has covered techniques of refunding, which lie at the heart of the Super Coupon Shopping System. These techniques are summarized on the next page.

Step-Three Summary

1. **Refunding provides three types of benefits.** Refunders receive cash, coupons, and gifts from manufacturers.

2. **Find offers and forms.** Refunding is a source of income based upon response to specific manufacturer offers. Learn of the offers from the six sources listed in this chapter.

3. **Create refunding triple plays.** Combine store sales with coupons and refund offers to realize the most complete savings possible. But always remember to buy only the products you will use.

4. **Save qualifiers, cash register tapes, and forms.** Determine how much time you're willing to spend and collect as thoroughly as that time allotment allows.

5. **Qualifiers can be any part of a package.** To maximize refund savings, you have to save almost every part of a product's package.

6. **Consider a limited collection of qualifiers.** Effective refunding can be accomplished by saving only proof of purchase seals, UPC symbols, and net weight statements.

7. **Organize everything that is saved.** Alphabetize qualifiers by brand name, keep CRTs accessible, track the expiration dates of forms. Consider keeping a refunding log.

8. **Regularly send out completed refund requests; send for forms; communicate with other refunders.** Refunds come regularly only if they are requested regularly. Space out addressing chores over the course of each month. Remember the need to also collect forms and information about offers.

9. **Comply with rebate offer terms.** Send exactly the qualifiers called for in the offer and remember to send them before expiration dates come due.

Shoppers' Networks

--- ✄

Super Shoppers recognize that the complexity of shopping in the modern world requires that we take a professional approach to the process. We research costs, gather and organize materials, and plot careful purchase strategies. We also, like other professionals, share information among ourselves to enhance the ability to succeed in our objective: realizing substantial savings, if not actual profits, from our shopping.

Our means of sharing that information is a bit different from the methods used by lawyers, doctors, and accountants. We don't print up and exchange business cards as in the networking rituals engaged in by these professionals (although if we could find a way to use a triple play in getting them printed, we might consider it). Our networks take the forms of newsletters, clubs, and conventions.

Our Own Newsletters

Refunding newsletters have been around a long time. The first appears to have been a few stapled, mimeographed sheets distributed by Niles Eggleston of Milford, New York, in 1954, named, hopefully, *Quick Silver* and containing information about refund offers. In the almost forty years since that humble beginning, hundreds of similar newsletters have sprouted and flourished for varying periods of time.

Most of these were simple, home-based operations begun by ordinary consumers seeking to extend their ability to shop for extraordinary values. Today there are about ten of these newsletters spread across the country, some serving primarily regional audiences. They share a subscription base of about 150,000, with perhaps four times as many other people also reading each copy.

Refunders, who by definition are close-fisted with their money, subscribe to these newsletters for one very simple reason: The newsletters provide information about offers and materials that permit refunders to save large amounts of money, amounts far larger than are saved by non-subscribers.

The information provided by newsletters is comprehensive and very useful. They list current rebate offers, provide forums in which refunders can trade forms and/or qualifiers, and provide areas in which people can discuss incidental details (like procedures for removing and storing qualifiers). Some newsletters devote themselves exclusively to offering lists or trades; others provide a mix of all three services.

The base of their success is their readers. Newsletters succeed because they draw upon the collected knowledge of all those who subscribe. As I discussed in the previous chapter, most refund offers are quite poorly publicized. Even avid refunders, who collect *everything*, will probably miss out on 90 percent of all offers if they don't subscribe to newsletters. Newsletter editors canvass the country, relying especially on reader information, to locate refund offers.

Many refund offers are publicized only in particular

regions, although the company will honor refund requests filed from anywhere in the country. Companies might narrowly limit publicity of an offer simply because their marketing research shows that in certain parts of the country their product sells less well than in others. So the companies try to boost sales in those areas through promotions that include refunds. Through *our* network, we learn of these regional opportunities and make use of them throughout the United States. After all, why should shoppers be discriminated against just because they live in an area where a product is popular?

The value of these listed offers can be substantial. A recent edition of *Refundle Bundle*, the bimonthly bulletin I publish, contained listings of almost 500 different rebate offers worth over seven hundred dollars. That is over seven hundred dollars in cash, coupons, and gifts (primarily cash) available to shoppers savvy enough to know of the offers and to have the materials on hand necessary to meet the offers' requirements.

The other great service provided by newsletters is in offering people in entirely different parts of the country the opportunity to trade forms and qualifiers.

The switch-and-swap feature of newsletters is particularly important to people in two circumstances. A shopper may have acquired forms for rebates on products she doesn't use, say pet food for a household with no pets. The same shopper, if a true Super Shopper, also has numerous qualifiers stuck in her filing boxes awaiting forms that will allow their return to the manufacturer. She'll attempt to trade her pet food form to someone who has a form matching her needed qualifiers. Each is then able to profit from the manufacturer's offer.

Another ingenious switch-and-swap occurs when a shopper fulfills the terms of an offer and retains enough qualifiers and forms to meet the offer requirements again, but is prevented by the common restriction limiting each household to one refund per offer. She may seek out another similarly situated shopper whose extra refund package is for another offer. They trade packages, and again both benefit.

Meeting Other Refunders

This sharing of information doesn't occur only through newsletters. Many refunders meet in clubs and conventions. In fact, these clubs, usually rather humbly organized by individual shoppers, have often been the spur to the development of regional and local newsletters.

A refund group may consist of as few as two people who meet occasionally to share information, forms, and deals. Obviously, though, as with newsletters, the sharing is more successful when there is a larger pool from which to pick. Refunders often try to expand the group, usually limiting it, for practical reasons, to about fifteen.

The group usually meets at the home of one of the refunders, rotating the meeting place monthly among their members. Members bring their forms, qualifiers, and coupons. After a period of socializing and sharing of refunding anecdotes and company information, people begin an organized process of trading their materials, continuing until everyone is finished. Some groups try to keep a record of anecdotal refunding information, such as which offers will be accepted without forms, which companies will mail forms to refunders upon request, which are more likely to repeat offers, and which tend to be prompt in making payments.

How to Begin

To start a club or organize a meeting, plan the initial meeting for a weekday night (when people are less likely to attend other events). Publicize the meeting by posting notices on community bulletin boards at the local library and at supermarkets. The notices should explain the purpose of the club (to share refunding information and materials); request that people bring coupons, forms, and qualifiers for trading; note that novices are welcome and that refunding will be explained to them; give the date and time of the meeting; and contain your phone number. As people call in response to the notices, write down their names, addresses, and phone numbers in preparation for creating a club roster.

At the first meeting, explain your purpose in arranging the meeting, and briefly explain the refunding process to those who are new. Most people will be enthusiastic and willing to share information about some of their refunding experiences and about opportunities they know of, such as supermarkets doubling coupons, locations of forms, and store specials.

Now you are ready to begin trading. To start, discuss and arrange some rules to govern the process. Generally, forms and coupons in categories will be exchanged on an even basis; one detergent coupon is worth one other detergent coupon. Otherwise, trading can take forever if people attempt to match up the face values of their coupons and forms. But allow exceptions to this rule where the coupon or form has a high face value or is rare or otherwise unusually valuable. The general rule is just that everyone should feel that they were treated fairly. Trades of full package refunds (qualifiers and forms), known as complete cash deals, should be done on an equal-value basis.

Begin trading by focusing on coupons and forms. The
easiest way to trade is to establish a list of categories and
work through one category at a time. Have each person, in
turn, announce what she has to trade in that category and
what she seeks in it. Others respond by making the trades.
Next have people announce the complete cash deals they
wish to trade, and then conclude the trades. When the
trading is complete and everyone is satisfied, don't forget
to arrange the time and location of the next meeting. The
whole evening will take two to three hours, everyone
should go home financially enriched, and all will have had
a pleasant night out.

Conventions

Conventions are worlds unto themselves, worlds created by
and for refunders. They are large all-day meetings of
refunders whose purpose is the exchange of materials and
information. As editor of *Refundle Bundle*, I've been invit-
ed to several to speak on panel discussions on the refunding
process. A Houston, Texas, convention I attended several
years ago is representative.

It was organized by three local refunders who gained
use of the city's American Legion Hall. In return, the hall
would realize profits through serving meals to the atten-
dees. The organizers contacted supermarkets, manufacturers, and refund experts to speak before the convention,
acquiring not only speakers but also bags full of sample
foods, newsletters, coupons, and other promotional items
distributed by these speakers. Over 500 people attended
the event.

We had fun and we made money. The first evening of
the convention was spent in informal trading sessions.

Refunders milled around large tables, letting one another look through shoe boxes filled with qualifiers and coupons that were traded on a one-for-one basis. I left the session with about $200 worth of cash-offs, forms, and qualifiers that I'd be able to use within the next few months.

The next day, Saturday, began with talks delivered by various representatives of the food industry, providing even me with new information. One food broker, for instance, told us that when they're stocking their products in a store, they often welcome approaches from customers to whom they will give coupons and samples. Following these talks were panel discussions that included spirited question-and-answer sessions. The day concluded with a buffet dinner spiced by everyone's tales of refunding and coupon success, and another informal trading session.

Most of us left the convention with hundreds of dollars in useful qualifiers gained from trading, scores of new coupons, a range of new acquaintances, and almost twenty dollars' worth of groceries given away by the stores and companies represented at the event. All in all, a very pleasant and profitable weekend.

Sharing the Wealth: Four Types of Trades

Trades let two consumers profit from offers that they each would otherwise lose out on. Trades can be divided into four categories: the cash-off deal, the form exchange, the qualifier exchange, and complete deals.

In the *cash-off deals,* refunders will offer to trade a certain number of cash-off coupons. Usually the offer will describe the type of cash-offs by category and note the general expiration date period on them. In return for these cash-offs, the refunder might request a handling fee (such as $1 for 20 cereal no-expiration coupons), other coupons, or a hard-to-find form.

In a *form exchange*, a refunder will usually offer or request specific forms, noting what they'd like in compensation. More commonly, advertisers offer a "potluck" assortment of forms in return for either money (usually $1 for fifty forms), cash-offs, or a similar grabbag of assorted forms.

As with forms and cash-offs, a *qualifier exchange* is the exchange of qualifiers for either money, forms, cash-offs, or other qualifiers. These offers are also made either as grab-bag assortments or by product name.

The *complete deals,* known also as complete package deals and complete cash deals, are trades between refunders of everything necessary to complete refund offers. The package contains the form and all necessary qualifiers. These deals are traded on a dollar-for-dollar basis; where one refunder offers a three-dollar complete cash deal, he expects to receive back some combination of complete cash deals also worth three dollars.

The practical effect of these deals is to avoid the cost of the one-per-family restriction attached to most refund offers. A regular user of Campbell's soups will have a lot of Campbell's qualifiers but only a limited number of refund opportunities. In this case, she may trade her extra qualifiers and forms for other complete cash deals as she chooses.

Frankly, companies are not particularly enamored of these kinds of trades. Usually the purpose of their refund plans is to encourage people to begin trying their products; exchanges effectively reward the shoppers who are loyal consumers of the company's products, and companies are not interested in furnishing such rewards. They believe that if they have long since established your loyalty, rewarding it is not something in which they've got a financial interest.

The trades—and redemptions—of complete deals do, however, comply with the letter of company rules. The products *are* purchased, and only one redemption is being accomplished per family. The spirit of the company rules may well be that rewards are to go only to new users of their products, but the spirit of Super Shopping is to gain all the benefits that are legitimately available. In any case, the companies do still realize some of their promotional goals by creating the goodwill established when refunders receive their rebates.

Although a fair amount of trading occurs through clubs and conventions, by far the greatest number of traders are brought together by newsletters. Since most of these relationships occur only through the mail, the standard governing them is one of trust. The trades in which these people engage are, as I've described, capable of including just about anything for just about anything. The principle governing all these transactions is, simply, that both parties be treated fairly. Generally, the monitoring role played by newsletter editors is to prohibit use of their newsletters by those few advertisers who fail to live up to the terms of their trades. For the most part, however, traders treat each other with honesty and respect.

Refundle Bundle: A Newsletter's Contents

In the forty years since *Quick Silver* appeared on the scene, numerous newsletters have been created by refunders who understood other refunders' need for information. Unfortunately, most of these bulletins have had short lives, in part because their founders were unprepared for treating them as the full-time jobs they become when they are successful. *Refundle Bundle* has a different story.

When I began *Refundle Bundle* over twenty years ago, my husband and I had decided that refunding could provide us with the income necessary to help two struggling teachers meet the mortgage payments of the new house we had purchased in anticipation of beginning a family. The initial *Refundle Bundle* contained six mimeographed sheets distributed to thirteen friends.

Within three years, in part because I was able to dedicate time to promoting the newsletter, my subscription base had neared one thousand. I had also given birth to my first son and had resigned my teaching position to stay home with the baby. I used my time at home to focus on the newsletter, considering and treating it as an important, income-producing job.

The commitment has paid off, creating a remarkably stable newsletter in such a transient field. Hundreds of thousands of people from across the United States have subscribed to *Refundle Bundle*. Many of these subscribers joined after seeing me on one of the many television shows on which I have appeared. Others have joined on the recommendation of subscribers, and still others have subscribed when similar newsletters have stopped publishing.

Each issue now contains about forty-eight pages, is printed professionally (no more ink-smeared papers and rags cluttering up the garage), and is mailed out by second class postage. *Refundle Bundle* contains elements typical of the surviving newsletters, providing the savings-dedicated services that the refunding network requires.

The three things refunders most desire from a newsletter (listings of offers, exchange advertisements, and general information) all appear within *Refundle Bundle*'s twelve sections.

Listings of Offers

Each issue includes alphabetical listings of offers new to that issue, which are not repeated from prior issues. Under the heading "Write for Forms," there is a listing of offers, containing the offers' requirements and the manufacturers' addresses, for which the companies will send forms upon request. In addition, there is the "No Form Needed," an alphabetical listing of offers that require, along with the qualifiers, only statements of the refund expected, the qualifiers included, and the refunder's name and address. There are also "Form Required Offers," which are all offers for which a form is required, containing information about sources of forms, amount and type of refunds, qualifiers needed, and expiration dates. This section is the largest section in each issue, usually containing information about more than 300 offers. Unique to *Refundle Bundle* is the "Procter & Gamble" listing. This corporation has a special section in each issue, befitting its status as the refunders' favorite company, because of its numerous promotions, its extreme courtesy and flexibility in dealing with refunders, and the promptness of its responses. Last, but not least, is the "Specially Marked Packages" section. This lists the products containing refund orders on packages.

Exchange Advertisements

Refundle Bundle also offers a "Qualifier Exchange," in which volunteers coordinate lists of qualifiers for products that can be exchanged on an equal basis (one Crest UPC for one Hershey's Syrup UPC). Using the list, participants in these swaps send the qualifiers they would like to exchange to the coordinator with a list of those qualifiers they would like to receive in return. The coordinator works out the trades and mails the requested qualifiers back in envelopes that the recipient has already stamped and addressed.

In addition, we do try to have coordinators handle exchanges of short-dated forms (those due to expire soon) and complete cash deals. I also include here the "Switch & Swap" section, in which refunders arrange their trades of cash-offs, forms, and qualifiers.

Information

Information about collecting, organizing, and storing qualifiers can always be found in the "Questions, Tips, and Ideas" section. This includes notes about free items and other deals available from companies and the government that are sent in by readers.

There is a sort of gossipy editorial page called "Tidbits," consisting primarily of notes from readers about the treatment, usually quite generous, they've received from companies when a mistake has been made by either the refunder or a clearinghouse. "Tidbits" is a good source of information about the methods used by different companies in relating to their customers. "On the Newsy Side" is a column containing brief discussions of new products and information about the grocery business. "The Select Coupon Program" contains information about buying and selling coupons in bulk quantities; I will explain this program more thoroughly in Step Six. "Explanations of Refunding Terms" is a glossary of the abbreviations used by refunders throughout the pages of *Refundle Bundle*.

Participation

Good refunding newsletters succeed only when their readers actively participate in their functions. *Refundle Bundle* draws on its subscriber base in a number of ways.

Two of those ways are obvious from the newsletter's exchange section. Readers have to actively advertise their interest in trades, and readers have to respond to those advertisements. Other readers have to volunteer to coordinate qualifier exchanges.

Readers are also sources of information in, especially, the tidbits and questions sections.

Finally, readers participate by keeping the magazine up to date with information about manufacturer offers. Refunders are requested to provide information about new offers and about official expirations of undated offers. Those who do will receive their choice of subscription extensions or cash payments for each tip they are the first to send in. These incentives basically create for *Refundle Bundle* a network of tens of thousands of reporters spread across the country who alert the newsletter to the latest changes in refunding.

I've discussed only *Refundle Bundle* here not to disparage any of the other bulletins, but because I feel that it is representative of what these newsletters do and because it is the one with which I have the greatest familiarity. Other newsletters certainly do a fine job; refunders should decide which newsletter best serves their needs.

Those interested in subscribing should write *Refundle Bundle*, P.O. Box 140, Centuck Station, Yonkers, NY 10710. A subscription, for twelve bimonthly issues, costs $19.87.

Regardless of which newsletter you choose to subscribe

to, absolute success in refunding is dependent on joining the refunding network. Step Four, which is all about joining, is summarized in the following five points:

Step-Four Summary

1. **Meet with other refunders.** Join, start, or attend clubs and conventions. Even finding only one other refunder will greatly increase your awareness of opportunities and ability to take advantage of trades of refund materials.
2. **Subscribe to a newsletter.** There is no better source of information on offers and possible trades.
3. **Trade with other refunders.** Use your personal and newsletter contacts. Swapping of forms, qualifiers, and even complete offers is perfectly legitimate.
4. **Provide information.** Newsletters and clubs are always seeking information about new and expired offers. People who provide the information are usually rewarded, and they certainly form the bedrock of the refunding community.
5. **Most refunders deal with each other honestly.** One of the pleasures in refunding-trade relationships is finding that most of the people involved are respectful of each other and don't try to cheat other refunders in their deals. We also find most companies treat us with great courtesy. In general, refunding is a pretty nice "profession" in which to engage.

Gifts Every Day

--- ✂

Refunders love getting their cash, checks, and coupons in the mail. We also, like most people, enjoy getting gifts. Unlike non-refunders, limited to receiving gifts on holidays and birthdays, we can virtually assume that we'll receive gifts in the mail throughout the year. The icing on the refunding cake is the premiums sent to us by manufacturers.

Types of Free Gifts

Although most refunders think the best gift is the one that gives them the most options for its use (money), others put their energies most fully into the acquisition of these manufacturers' giveaways. There are refunders whose entire kitchens seem to have been stocked by corporate America. Dishes, utensils, shelves of cookbooks, and even dishtowels arrive in their kitchens via the U. S. Mail. And the kitchen is not the only room that can be outfitted with premiums.

My family, without really trying, has acquired from manufacturers hundreds of free gifts that are scattered throughout the house. The boys' rooms are loaded. There are baseball cards, baseballs, cassette tapes, sunglasses, T-shirts, pro-football team hats, books, and maps. In the attic we still have wonderful toys from when they were younger. Great hardcover books, shovels and pails, a wagon, puppets, and a shelf full of Fisher-Price toys were all manufacturers' gifts.

The list could go on and on. A comprehensive list would run ten pages, and the value of all the premiums we've received must run into the thousands of dollars. Granted, some of these things I would never have spent money on, but that is exactly the point—they're gifts, and I don't have to worry whether I should or shouldn't purchase them. All I have to give up are some qualifiers, and those I give up for premiums are invariably qualifiers I have in quantity.

Basically, premium giveaways operate in much the same fashion as do other refunds. A product is purchased and the qualifiers are saved. The manufacturer offers the premium in return for a specified number of qualifiers. The consumer learns of the premium offer, sends in the qualifiers to a clearinghouse address, and, within weeks, receives his new video, dessert plate, lunch bag, mug, or stuffed animal.

Four-Way Savings

The best way to get premiums is to keep in mind that their only cost to you is the value of the qualifiers used to receive them. Those qualifiers have two values: the cost of the product from which they came and their opportunity worth, that is, what other refunds the qualifiers could be used to obtain. I like to reduce these costs by using premium offers to achieve four-way savings.

What I try to do is to purchase the products on sale using coupons that are doubled. I then try to limit my premium refunds to those items I can buy in bulk, either because they have long shelf lives or because my family uses large quantities of the products. This bulk-buying gives me a large number of qualifiers, which lessens the likelihood that I'll be able to use all of them for cash refunds.

An example would be Energizer batteries. Periodically, coupons are printed for these and, just as periodically, the stores put them on sale. My store reduced the prices of these to $1.59 and $1.79 per package, down from $2.19

Premium order forms

and $2.39. I had ten 50-cents-off coupons that, when doubled, reduced the price to 59 and 79 cents per package, already saving me sixteen dollars on the ten packages (which my four sons can go through in a matter of weeks). So, I've already achieved two parts of my savings by using my coupons and by taking advantage of the dual store promotions of sale prices and double coupons.

The last two parts of my savings occur through refunding. I use four of the qualifiers to gain a two-dollar rebate. The other six are sent to an Illinois address for a "Cool Energizer Bunny T-Shirt," which one of us will have great fun wearing. So, we get batteries, and get them cheap, we get money in the mail, and we get a nice-quality T-shirt. Four-way savings.

Who's Embarrassed?

People sometimes ask me if I'm embarrassed to wear and use company "promo" items. Others are convinced that we shape our shopping habits around promotional offers, forcing us to use products we would otherwise shun.

Well, we do shop with our eyes focused on one critical promotional feature: paying the lowest prices for the best products. My family is probably less likely, in fact, to accept distasteful products than are the families of normal shoppers, because my family is not artificially bound by brand loyalties. We try new things when they're worth trying. Nevertheless, we always abide by one of the Super Shopper's cardinal rules: Don't buy what you don't need. And we most certainly don't "need" anything that we find distasteful.

As far as being embarrassed goes, I've made a pretty nice career out of demonstrating the benefits of my kind of shopping. And I don't see anything embarrassing about using good-quality materials that I can get, legally, for free. In fact, I take some pride in it.

It's also amusing, I think, that it has become fashionable to buy shirts that have company logos printed on them. I think it's a lot less embarrassing to wear a Cool Energizer Bunny T-Shirt that I got free than it is to wear a T-shirt of the same-quality cotton for which I've paid twenty dollars to advertise the name of a manufacturer boldly emblazoned across the shirt. It sure seems like a pretty good deal for the manufacturer to have someone pay to advertise their products. The way I see it, my premiums only show that I save money, and enjoy doing it. What could possibly be embarrassing about that?

Cash-Plus Deals

Cash-plus, or money-plus, deals are arrangements where manufacturers offer premiums in return for a combination of cash and qualifiers. Sometimes these deals are offered as options, with the premium available for either a large number of qualifiers or for a smaller number of qualifiers, with the reduction compensated for by some amount of cash.

To most refunders, these deals are anathema. Premiums are supposed to be gifts; merchandise for which one has to pay money quickly loses the label of gift. For the most part, I avoid cash-plus offers, and even keep them out of the offers listed in *Refundle Bundle* because I believe that they, by requiring payments of cash, run counter to the thrust of the newsletter. Of course, there are no absolutes; occasionally even I will find a cash-plus offer to be a genuine deal that I'll purchase. But, even with a good deal, it still feels more like a purchase, admittedly at a discount, then it does a genuine refund.

These offers are somewhat different from those premium offers that request postage-and-handling fees to be submitted along with the qualifiers. It is becoming increasingly common for manufacturers to request these fees for delivery of their premiums. These fees, however, are beginning to seem less nominal and more like a significant cost to be factored in when considering whether or not to redeem the premium offer. With postage-and-handling fees regularly reaching $2, the difference between cash-plus deals and deals requiring postage and handling seems more semantic than real.

Points Clubs

Point coupon systems are promotions in which the consumer purchases items from the club catalog by redeeming points accumulated from a manufacturer's products. Often these catalog items are available for either points alone or for a cash-plus deal. The most well known point system is General Mills' Betty Crocker coupon plan.

The plan has its virtues in that the items are good quality and they are free, relatively. The cost of this and other plans is the hidden price known as an "opportunity cost." Every POP used to accumulate Betty Crocker points is one less opportunity to receive other refunds. A shopper blindly set on accumulating catalog points is likely to overlook cash-back refunds, which may actually have greater value than the premiums acquired through the catalog.

Other points clubs have greater value because the value of their POPs is more limited. These situations are more likely to occur with things such as toys. One example is the club established by Mattel for purchasers of Barbie Dolls and supplies. These POPs have little other use and seem well suited

POP from one of the Salon Selectives product: (punch out the pop disc from the top of tha cap for:) Mousse, Styling Spritz, or Aerosol Hairspray; (out the UPC from the back of the box or packet for:) Hot Oil Treatment; (write the UPC# for:) Shampoo, Conditioner, Non-Aerosol Hairspray, Gsl, Volumizing Spray, Leave-In Conditioner, Perfect Curls, Spray Gel, or Style Freeze.
SS 8/31/93

SCOOP AWAY REBATE OFFER, Dept. 921658, Lubbock, TX 79491-1658. $3.00. Send 3 POPs from 3 Scoop Away products.
SS ED

SEALTEST/MILTON BRADLEY REBATE,OFFER, P.O.Box 52992, Dept. 1652, Phoenix, AZ 85072-2993. $1.00 per game, limit $10.00. Send, for each $1.00 requested, CRTC dated between 5/1/93-9/30/94 + 1 UPC from the game box of any Milton Bradley Travel Game + the UPC from any -gallon of Sealtest Ice Cresm.
SS 10/15/94

SECURITY REFUNDS, P.O.Box 52979, Dept. 1533, Phoenix, AZ 85072-2979. $2.00 per different product, limit 4-(up to $8.00). Send, for each product submitted, CRTC te ermdedl"bee UPC from the labelof any of the following Security Brands products: Diazinon Spray, Malathion Spray, Sevin Spray, Lawn Weed Killer (quart size). LTD: PA,NY,NJ,DE,& MD.
SF 8/31/93

SENOKOT LAXATIVES GIFT CERTIFICATE, PF, P.O.Box 7777, C30, Dept. 18, Mt. Prospect, IL 60056-7777. .t.$25Qd Send CRTC + the UPC from a pckg of Senokot Tablets 20s or SenokotXta Tablets 12s- get $1.00, or from a pckg of Senokot Tablets 100s or 50s or from Senokot-S Tablets 60s or 30s- get $2.00.
SF 33194

SENSODYNE $1.00 REFUND, P.O.Box 7919, Clinton, IA 52736. $1.00. Send CRTC + the UPC from 1 carton of Sensodyne Toothpaste: (Fresh Mint, Cool Gel, or Original Formula SC).
SF 3/31/94

SERENITY FREE SAMPLE PACK OFFER, P.O.Box 5234, Clifton, NJ 07015-5234. Free sample pack o 2 Serenity Guards. Send completed form.
HM 2/28/94

SHADY BROOK FARMS, P.O.Box 113-B, Bridgewater, VA 22812. $5/$10 off or a free Shady Brook Farms Turkey. Send CRTC(s) dated between 5/23/93-9/30/93 + the product labels from any Shady Brook Farms fresh turkey products. Send 10 labels + CRTC(s)- get $5.00 off a Shady Brook Farms turkey, send 20 labels- get $10.00 off, send 30 labels- get cpn for a free Shady Brook Farms turkey.
SS 930/93

SHOWER TO SHOWER $1.50 REFUND OFFER, P.O.Box 8253, Dept. A, Young America, MN 55551-8253. $1.50. Send dated CRTC(s) + the ellow "With Cornstarch" sticker from the cap of 1 Shower To Shower Antiperspirant + write the UPC# from 1 Shower To Shower Body Powder.
SF 12/31/93

(SLIM FAST) ULTRA SLIM-FAST FRUIT JUICE MIX REBATE, P.O.Box 8922, Young America, MN 55551-8922. Up to $5.00. Send CRTC + the UPC from 1 Ultra Slim Fast Fruit Juice Mix Powder canister label.
SF 11/30/93

(SLIM-FAST) ULTRA SLIM-FAST $3.00 PLUS REBATE, P.O.Box 8934, Young America, MN 55551-8934. $3.00. Send CRTC + the UPC from 1 Ultra Slim-Fast Plus Powder canister label.
SF 7/31/93

(SMA/NURSOY) WYETH FREE BABY ITEM OFFER, P.O.Box 14312, Baltimore, MD 21268. Cpn for any brand baby shampoo, wipes or lotion-(up to $3.50l + $2.00 in SMA or Nursoy cpns. Send CRTC(s) write the UPC# from the side of can from 6 cans (13 fl.oz) of Concentrated Liquid or 6 cans (32 fl. oz) or Ready To Feed or 2 cans (16-oz or larger) of Powder o SMA Infant Formula or Nursoy Soy Protein Formula.
SF 12/15/93

SMUCKER'S $2.00 OFF ICE CREAM OFFER, P.O.Box 3000, Dept. ICT3, Medina, OH 44258-3000. $2.00 cpn for ice cream. Send the net weiht statements from 2 jars or bottles of SMucker's Ice Cream Toppings: (Regular, Special Recipe, Magic Shell or Squeeze bottle) + the brand name from a gallon or larger container of ice cream.
SF 12/3193

SMUCKER'S FREE WALNUTS OFFER, P.O.Box 3000, Dept. WN, Medina, OH 44258-3000. Cpn for free walnuts-(up to $1.50). Send the net weight statement from 1 jar of Smucker's Ice Cream Topping + the UPC from one 6-oz or larger pckg of walnuts + a % gallon or larger container of ice cream.
SF 9/30/93

SOMETHING BETTER! $1 REBATE OFFER, Dept. 561, P.O.Box 8708, Newport Beach, CA 92658-9873. $1.00. Send CRTC dated between 4/1/93-12/31/93 + write the UPC from one 15-oz can of Something Better! Foam Protectant.
SF 1/15/94

SNACKER REFUND OFFER, P.O.Box 440106, El Paso, TX 88544-0106. $$1.00. Send store named & dated CRTC(s) + the UPC from 2 pckges of Snacker 40 ct or greater.
SF 1/31/94

SON OF GUN! REFUND OFFER, P.O.Box 7067, Clinton, IA 52736. Up to $2.00. Send CRTC(s)-with the price of one 8-oz or 10-oz Son Of A Gun! Protectant- get $1.00, and/or a 16-oz or 20-oz Son Of A Gun! Protectant- get 2.00. Limit one $1.00 and one $2.00 refund.
SF 9/30/93

S.O.S. KITCHEN SAFE $1.50 REFUND OFFER, P.O.Box 6401, Douglas, AZ 85655-6401. $1.50. Send dated CRTC + write the UPC# from one S.O.S. Kitchen-Safe All Purpose Cleaner bottle.
SF 7/31/93

SPENCO 2nd SKIN MOIST BURN PADS OFFER, P.O.Box 1637, Ridgely, MD 21681. $1.00. Send dated CRTC + the UPC from any full size Spenco 2nd Skin Moist Burn Pads kg.
HM 12/31/93

(STAIN AWAY) REGET LABS, INC., REBAE XPESS, 700 W. Hillsboro Blvd., Bldg. 2, 206, Deerfield Beach, FL 33441. $2.00. Send a SAE + a Thrifty CRTC + the UPC from bottom of 1 box of Stain Away Plus.
SF 12/31/93

STAYFREE $1.00 REFUND OFFER, P.O.Box 697, Dept. 2002, Gibbstown, N3 08027. $1.00. Send CRTC + the UC from 1 box of Stayfree Maxi (48 ct.
SF 2/28/94

STAYFREE $3.29 REFUND OFFER, P.O.Box 12, Dept. 1550, Gibbstown, NJ 08027. $3.29. Send CRTC + the UPC from 1 box of Stayfree Ultra Thin Maxi or Stayfree Ultra Thin Plus Maxi Liner.
SF 2/28

(STOVE TOP) FREE RACING CAP, P.O.Box 23733, Kankakee, IL 60902-3733. Free Stove Top Racing Cap. Send 2 UPCs from two 24-oz pckges of Stove Top Stuffing Mix.
NF WSL

STP PERFORMANCE KIT REFUND OFFER, P.O.Box 6024, Douglas, AZ 85655-6024. $3.00. Send CRTC + the UPC from 1 box of STP Performance Kit.
SF 12/31/93

SUCCESS 32-oz REBATE OFFER, P.O.Box 801393, Houston, TX 77280-1393. $1.50. Send CRTC + the

for obtaining toys related to their original purchases.

Toys arriving in the mail do have a value beyond their usefulness as playthings. Children learn, through positive reinforcement, the virtues of being a discriminating, proactive shopper. They see that it is possible for individuals to manipulate systems that were designed to manipulate individuals. I think it teaches them small but powerful lessons about the way we can take control of our daily lives.

Trading Stamps

The final source of premiums is really a promotion run not by manufacturers but by retailers. Trading-stamp systems are quite similar to points clubs in that the consumer redeems premiums (here stamps), perhaps with cash, for gifts listed in catalogs.

Super Shoppers find a few problems with trading stamps. First is that the stores that offer them buy the stamps from the companies offering them. These costs are then passed along the way all other costs are passed along by retailers: directly to the consumer. Stores that offer trading stamps invariably charge higher prices than do the stores that don't.

The other critical problem with trading stamps is that consumers get locked into shopping at the stores that feature the programs. Filling one book and moving on to the next becomes more important than finding the store that offers the best deals. The stamp collector, unlike the Super Shopper, can find herself suddenly loyal to a store rather than to the best prices.

For those shoppers with books of trading stamps gathering dust, the following lists of companies that still redeem their stamps and of companies who have gone out of business, rendering their stamps unredeemable, may be helpful. Check the reference section of your local library for the addresses of active companies.

Still Redeemable

Affiliated Merchantile Circle W
    Blue Stamps
Big Bonus Stamp Co.
Blue Chip Stamp Co.
Buckeye Premium Stamps, Inc.
Community Savings Stamp Co.
Consumers Reserve Green
    Stamp Corp.
Consumers Trading Stamp
    Corp.
Eagle Stamp Co.
Family Stamp Co.
Gold Bond Stamp Co.
Gold Strike
Greenbax Stamp Co.

Gunn Bros. Thrift Stamp Co.
Holden Red Stamp Co.
International United Industries
E. F. MacDonald Stamp Co.
    (Plaid)
Mor-Valu Stamps
Quality Stamp Co.
Regal Stamp Co.
S&H Green Stamps
Shur-Valu Stamps, Inc.
Teruya Bros. Royal Stamps
Texas Gold Stamp Co.
Top Value Enterprises, Inc.
Vest Promotions
    (Dollar Stretcher)

No Longer Redeemable

Bonus Gifts
Consumer's Profit Sharing
F. S. Gold Stamps
Food Fair Inc., Merchant's
    Green Stamps
Gift House Stamp Co.
King Korn Stamp Co.
National Red

NY Yellow Stamp Co.
Philadelphia Yellow
Pot-O-Gold Stamp Co.
"Q" Yellow Stamp Co.
Thrifty Green
Triple-S
United Savings Stamps
World Green Stamps

Super Shoppers can have it all. We can get bargains at the market, and we can get both money *and* gifts in the mail. To receive premiums, follow the guidelines of Step Five, summarized in the following four points:

Step-Five Summary

1. **Good quality merchandise is available free to those who send for it.** The process used to acquire premiums is the same as in other forms of refunding.
2. **Try to gain four-way savings.** Use qualifiers wisely when redeeming premiums offers. Try to gain savings in the store with coupons, and through cash rebates before redeeming qualifiers for gifts, unless the gifts have some special value to you.
3. **Enjoy your premiums.** You earned them through your understanding and handling of the system. Your acquisitions are things to be proud of.
4. **Be wary.** Consider the value of cash-plus deals. Don't let yourself become blindly loyal to any of the catalog systems run by manufacturers and trading stamp companies.

The Select Coupon Program

--- ✂

This is the part of the Super Coupon Shopping System that provokes the greatest amount of disbelief. Many people are certain that selling coupons is somehow a criminal enterprise, the type of thing engaged in by people wearing long trench coats in which to hide the evidence of their transactions. Well, there is nothing wrong with selling coupons so that people can use them for product discounts.

It is true that some cash-offs contain a statement claiming that the coupon is void if transferred. Now, "transferring" occurs constantly (between friends and relatives and through exchange boxes maintained by supermarkets and libraries, for example), and I've never heard of such transferred coupons failing to be honored. Additionally, I have no knowledge of any federal or state statute that prohibits the transfer of coupons in a free-market society. However, the statement may give manufacturers the legal right to refuse redemption of transferred coupons. Shoppers concerned about this should simply not use transferred coupons that contain such statements.

In the end, selling coupons appears to be perfectly legitimate. Probably all, and certainly most, coupons are simply commodities whose values are determined by the prices individuals are willing to pay for them in the free market.

Coupons by Choice, Not Chance

The potential free market for coupons is vast. There were about four hundred billion coupons, worth about two hundred billion dollars, distributed in 1992. Not only is the supply of coupons huge, but the demand for them comes from a similarly large group. Almost 80 percent of all American families use coupons at least occasionally. Yet, somehow, there is not a proper fit between coupon supply and public demand, because less than 4 percent of all coupons are actually redeemed.

The problem, of course, is that each coupon is limited to use on a specific product. The problem is intensified by the imperfect distribution of coupons. For the most part, people receive only the coupons that happen to reach them; shoppers have little opportunity to target themselves for delivery of the coupons they want to use. Coupons arrive almost entirely by chance.

Select Coupon Program

The one way that shoppers can get the coupons they wish to use is through membership in the Select Coupon Program. The program maintains coupons for over 1,000 different brand-name products that are cataloged and made available through distribution of selection lists. Members of the club receive the current selection list upon request and choose from it the coupons they want. The selection lists are updated monthly, reflecting changes in supply and in customer preference.

MEMBERSHIP FORM
SELECT COUPON PROGRAM
66 South Central Ave., Elmsford, NY 10523

Please send this membership form with a separate sheet of your coupon selections listed in numerical order.

Special Membership Offer!

❑   6 Months   reg. $15   only $9.95
              (You receive $10 in coupons *FREE!*)

❑   One Year   reg. $25   only $19.95
              (You receive $20 in coupons *FREE!*)

Service Fee: $6 for each $18 worth of
                   additional coupons you order $_____

Total: Payment is enclosed for the
                   membership fee plus the service fee $_____

Charge my: ❑ VISA   ❑ MasterCard

_____
CARD #   EXP. DATE

_____
SIGNATURE

_____
NAME

_____
ADDRESS

_____
CITY   STATE   ZIP

*Important: Be sure to enclose a long, self-addressed, stamped (52¢)
                    envelope (LSASE).*

INSTRUCTIONS:
1. Print your name and address on the above application.
2. Check whether you are joining for 6 months or for 1 year.
3. Enter the amount of "service fee" you are including ($6.00 service fee for
   $18.00 in coupons).
4. You will receive a Master Selection List and a Certificate good for the
   appropriate amount of coupons that you will be ordering.
5. Return this Certificate and your selections in numerical order with a long
   self-addressed stamped envelope (52¢).
6. Mail to Select Coupon Program, 66 S. Central Ave., Elmsford, NY 10523

Select Coupon Program membership form

OFFICIAL COUPON SUPPLIER PROGRAM APPLICATION FORM

NAME

ADDRESS

CITY   STATE   ZIP

PHONE

SIGNATURE

Official Coupon Supplier Program, *Check here*:

❏ One-Time Trial Need List—$7.50.

❏ One-Year Membership—$22.50 plus $2.50 for Need List.

(Include a long self-addressed stamped envelope with 52¢ postage.)

Send to: **Select Coupon Program**, 66 South Central Ave. Elmsford, NY 10523.

We make no claims as to how much you can earn. Earnings are determined by your efforts and your ability to gather and accumulate coupons. Good luck in this venture.

IMPORTANT: Do not send any coupons until you have received your Need List.

Official Coupon Supplier Program application form

PREFERRED COUPON SUPPLIER PROGRAM APPLICATION FORM

NAME

ADDRESS

CITY   STATE   ZIP

PHONE

SIGNATURE

❏ One-Time Trial List—$19.00. *(Include a long self-addressed stamped envelope with 52¢ postage.)*

❏ 6-Month Membership—$29.00 plus $9.00 each Need List. (Include 6 separate long self-addressed stamped envelopes with 52¢ postage on each one.).Total payment—$83.00.

Send to: **Select Coupon Program**, 66 South Central Ave. Elmsford, NY 10523.

IMPORTANT: Absolutely no refunds. We wish you the best of luck in this venture.

Preferred Coupon Supplier Program application form

Membership is open to anyone who pays the membership fee of $19.95 per year, for which they immediately receive coupons of value equal to the fee. Over the course of their membership, members can then order coupons off the selection lists, paying the program one-third of the face value of the coupons selected and received. All transactions occur in multiples of six dollars.

So a new member could pay the $19.95 membership fee and order eighteen dollars' worth of coupons for an additional six-dollar service fee. For $25.95, she'll receive thirty-eight dollars in coupons, which, if local stores double them, are worth seventy-six dollars. That's a potential savings, in the first month alone, of fifty dollars. All the coupons distributed are for products requested, they are all for the highest value on hand, and no more than five will be given (unless the member requests more) for each product.

Sample membership and application forms for the club appear on pages 115 and 116.

Selling to the Program

The Select Coupon Program is a highly effective way of supplying hundreds of billions of unused coupons to the millions of shoppers who would like to use them. You may very well be one source of these coupons. The club purchases all its coupons from people who go about the process of collecting them. To maintain its supply of coupons, the club has created two different programs for coupon suppliers of varying resources: the Official Coupon Supplier and the Preferred Coupon Supplier.

Each program is distinct and tailored to meet the abilities and capacities of different people. Most collectors, with a bit of patience and commitment, find that at least one of the programs is suited to them and a likely source of unanticipated coupon-generated money.

The Official Coupon Supplier

Official Coupon Suppliers receive commissions equal to 5 to 15 percent of the face value of the coupons they supply. These coupons *must* be the coupons that appear on Need Lists sent to the supplier.

Individuals become Official Coupon Suppliers by submitting a $22.50 annual computer processing and data entry fee. The fee permits the supplier to purchase Need Lists for $2.50 each, which provide the supplier with listings of those coupons the club will accept. Need Lists are revised between eight and ten times a year. One-time Trial Need Lists are available for $7.50 without payment of the annual fee to those who are uncertain if they want to fully enter the program.

The Official Coupon Supplier rules are as follows:

1. Coupons must be trimmed neatly on all four sides.

2. Coupons with cut-off expiration dates will not be accepted.

3. Military, commissary, and plastic coupons and coupons from labels and box tops will not be accepted.

4. All coupons must be sorted. There must be at least five for each product sent, and they must be bundled together. They may have different face values.

5. Do not send expired coupons.

6. Send *only* coupons which appear on the Need List. No others will be accepted.

7. All coupons must be received by the club no later than the date specified on the Need List. Late coupons will not be accepted.

8. Do not alter any coupons. Alterations of expiration dates or face values will result in disqualification from the club.

9. Do not separate coupons with staples, paper clips, or pieces of paper or cardboard.

10. Bundle all coupons tightly with rubber bands. A rule of thumb is to use one rubber band per inch of coupons.

11. Do not send coupons in regular mailing envelopes. Use sturdier containers such as cartons, boxes, and manila envelopes.

12. Send all coupons first class prepaid. Postage-due packages will be rejected.

Need Lists

The basis of successful supplying is strict adherence to the Need List. Each list contains requests for coupons for 500 to 650 different products. Each list also contains a date by which the coupons on the list must reach the club. This date is usually about one month after the date the list is issued.

The list will also require that all coupons have expiration dates no earlier than a given date, so that the club will be able to sort the coupons and distribute them to club members while the coupons are still valid. This date is usually at least thirty-four days after the date on which the coupons must arrive at the club.

Each item on the list is also marked to let the supplier know the maximum number of coupons that can be sent for the item. These ceilings are usually several hundred coupons.

Suppliers should remember that Need Lists are revised regularly, so coupons that are not requested one month may very well be needed in subsequent months. Unexpired coupons should be saved.

Preferred Coupon Supplier

This program is designed for the more advanced coupon supplier. It is a program that offers a higher return for coupons, but is more restrictive in its requirements.

This program pays 15 percent of the face value of all coupons sent in response to the Preferred Supplier Need List. These lists are sent monthly and contain coupon requests for only 150 different products.

The rules governing operation of this program are basically the same as the rules for the Official Supplier Program, with the additional restriction that no more than ten coupons may be sent for each product on the list.

High-Demand Coupons

There are certain products for which coupons are in fairly constant demand. Suppliers should always save coupons for these products, expecting that they will soon appear on a Need List.

First come any products manufactured by Procter & Gamble. P&G is the world's largest manufacturer of packaged goods, and the favorite company of refunders. There's a steady demand for their products, and, of course, for the coupons with which to gain savings on those products.

Following is a list of P&G products, arranged alphabetically by brand name:

Always	Cascade	Crush Soda
Biz	Charmin	Dash
Bold II	Cheer	Dawn
Bounce	Chloraseptic	Downy
Bounty	Citrus Hill Juice	Dreft
Camay Soap	Crest	Gain

Gleem
Head & Shoulders
High Point Coffee
Hires Soda
Ivory Liquid
Ivory Shampoo
Ivory Snow
Ivory Soap
Jif
Joy
Lestoil

Luvs
Mr. Clean
Oxydol
Pampers
Pepto-Bismol
Pert
Posh Puffs
Press
Pringles
Puffs
Puritan Oil

Safeguard Soap
Scope
Secret Deodorants
Solo
Sure Deodorants
Tender Leaf Tea
Tide
Top Job
White Cloud
Wondra Lotion
Zest Soap

In addition, here is a list of other popular products for which we have a fairly high demand for coupons:

Aim Toothpaste
Bisquick
Borden's American
   Cheese
Breyers Ice Cream
Brillo Pads
Brim
Campbell's Soups
Cheerios
Clorox Liquid
County
Cycle Dog Food
Del Monte Fruits
Del Monte Juice
   Drinks
Dole Juice Drinks
Dove Face Soap

Fleischmann's
   Margarine
Gerber Baby Foods
Hawaiian Punch
Heinz Baby Foods
Huggies
Imperial Margarine
Keebler Cookies
Kleenex Napkins
   and Tissues
Kool-Aid
Kraft American
   Cheese
Kraft Velveeta
Lender's Bagels
Lipton Tea Bags
Maxwell House

Milk Bone Products
Nabisco Products
Ore-Ida
Peter Pan
Rice Krispies
Sanka
Scott Towels and
   Napkins
Sealtest Ice Cream
Skippy
SOS Pads
Sunshine Cookies
Tampax Tampons
Tang
Tropicana
Viva
Windex

Organizing Coupons

Use a long box or series of boxes divided by cards labeled with product names and Select Coupon Program numbers. Place coupons behind the correct dividers and remove them as needed. With your coupons arranged in this fashion, you'll be able to immediately determine which of the Need List's hundreds of requests can be filled out of your collection.

Step Six of the Super Coupon Shopping System, summarized in the following five points, is the method by which Super Shoppers collect and sell extra coupons.

Step-Six Summary

1. **Selling Coupons is legal.** There's a huge market of coupons waiting to be matched with users. The Select Coupon Club gives coupon collectors the opportunity to sell their coupons so that users can obtain them.
2. **Become an official coupon supplier.** Join the club and earn 5 percent of the face value of the coupons you send in.
3. **Become a preferred coupon supplier.** Provide the club with certain select coupons for which you'll receive 15 percent of their face value.
4. **Be attentive to Need Lists, Master Lists, and those coupons for which high demand exists.** Keep valuable coupons and be sure to use them when the club calls for them.
5. **Organize your coupons.** Keep your club supplier coupons organized in a system that complements the club's method of requesting coupons.

This book has been my attempt to share my system. I hope that it succeeds in opening the doors to a marvelous world of savings for those who read it. Your entry into this world benefits not only you, but those of us already there. The more Super Shoppers we have, the greater the store of experience and knowledge from which we can all draw, and the more able we will be to take advantage of the money-saving opportunities that await us.

The Refunder's Glossary

This glossary lists the terms and abbreviations commonly used by refunders and couponers. It draws heavily upon the usage in *Refundle Bundle*; other newsletters may use additional terms, but these should suffice for an informed introduction to the field.

CB: Cardboard backing. The backing behind a pad of store refund forms, which usually contains a company contact address for a form or for the refund itself.

C/D: Complete deal or complete cash deal. An exchange in which two refunders trade "packages" of all the material, qualifiers, and forms needed to cash in on refunds.

C/O: Cash-off coupon. A certificate entitling its user to purchase an item at a specified discount. These are redeemed at retail stores.

CRT: Cash register tape. Sometimes required by manufacturers to accompany qualifiers for refund requests.

CRTC: Cash register tape circled. Request by manufacturer that qualifiers be accompanied by CRT, with the purchase price of the refunded item circled on the CRT.

DM: Direct mailer. Mail containing coupons, free samples, and/or forms sent directly to residences by manufacturers.

EPOP: Each pay own postage. Each partner to an exchange must cover his or her own postage costs.

Form: An order blank that must accompany qualifiers in some refund offers.

H/F: Handling fee. A charge required by some newsletter advertisers and by some manufacturers to cover costs of sending out forms, qualifiers, or premiums.

HM: Home mailer. *See* DM.

HT: Hang tag. A store form that is hung around the neck of a bottle or jar.

LSASE: Long self-addressed stamped envelope. *See* SASE.

LTD: Limited to a certain area. The advertised offer is restricted to a certain part of the country.

M/F: Magazine form. A refund order form found in a magazine.

Money-   An offer that requires cash, in addition to
plus: qualifiers, for successful redemption. Also called "cash-plus."

NED: No expiration date. The advertised offer has no set expiration date and thus may expire at any time.

NF: Newspaper form. A refund offer found in a newspaper.

NFN: No form needed. A refund offer that requires no form, only a statement of the offer, the refunder's name and address, and the proper qualifiers.

POP: Proof of purchase. The more restrictive use refers to parts of a package so labeled. Sometimes used to refer to any part of a package required to meet refund offers.

PP: Purchase price.

Qualifier: Any part of a package required to meet the terms of a refund offer. UPCs have become the most common qualifiers used, although manufacturers can and will use any part of a product's packaging.

REQ: Required. Indicating that a form is required to meet the terms of an offer.

Round Robin: A trading system in which refunders from different locations exchange forms, qualifiers, and coupons. Each member of the group removes what he or she needs from the circulating material and mails it on around the circle.

SASE: Self-addressed stamped envelope. Most exchanges require these so that refunders bear their own postage costs.

SF: Store form. A refund order form found in a store.

SMP: Specially marked package. A package that contains either a coupon or a refund order form.

SS: Sunday supplement. The advertising section of the newspaper, usually rife with coupons.

UPC: Universal product code. A series of lines over a code number that appears on most supermarket items. These have become the part of packages most likely to be used as refund qualifiers.

VD: Void in certain areas. *See* LTD.

WFF: Write for forms. Forms can be obtained by writing the manufacturer making the rebate offer.

WSL: While supplies last. The rebate offer can expire at any time once the resources dedicated to supporting it have been exhausted.

1-4-1:   One for one. An exchange where forms, coupons, or qualifiers are traded on an equal, per item basis, with no attention paid to the face values of the items.

National Brands to Save

Serious refunders should save qualifiers, forms, and coupons from the following brands. They will almost certainly have offers made on them within a reasonable period of time.

A-1	Booth	Clairol
Adolph's	Bounce	Clorox
Aim	Bounty	Colgate
Alka-Seltzer	Brach's	College Inn
Anacin	Breck	Comet
Appian Way	Breyers	Complete
Armour	Brim	Cremora
Aunt Jemima	Bryan	Crest
Axion	Bufferin	Crisco
Bachman	Buitoni	Cudahy
Bacos	Bush	Curad
Baggies	Butter Nut	Cutex
Bauer & Black	Campbell's	Cycle
Bayer	Carnation	Del Monte
Beechnut	Cascade	Dermassage
Best Foods	Celeste	Diet Rite
Betty Crocker	Charmin	Dixie Crystals
Birds Eye	Cheerios	Dove
Bisquick	Chef Boy-ar-dee	Dow
Biz	Chex	Downy
Blue Bonnet	Chips Ahoy	Dr Pepper
Bold	Chun King	Drakes

Duncan Hines
Duracell
Dynamo
Eagle Brand
Ehlers
Era
Eveready
Fab
Final Touch
Flintstones
Folgers
Franco-American
Fresca
Frito-Lay
Gaines
Gala
General Mills
Gerber
Gillette
Glad
Glass Magic
Good Seasons
Green Giant
Greenwood
Hamburger
 Helper
Handiwipes
Handi-wrap
Hanover
Hawaiian Punch
Head & Shoulders
Hefty

Heinz
Hellman's
Hershey's
Hidden Valley
Holloway House
Howard
 Johnson's
Hunts
Hygrade
Ivory
Jell-O
Jeno's
Jergens
JFG
Johnson &
 Johnson
K2R
Kellogg's
Kimbies
Kingsford
Kleenex
Kool-Aid
Kordite
Kotex
Kraft
Land O'Lakes
L'Oréal
Lender's
Lipton
Listerine
Lysol
M&M/Mars

Marcal
Maxwell House
Mazola
Minute Maid
Mueller's
Nabisco
Nestlé
Palmolive
Pampers
Pepperidge Farm
Purina
Ragu
Rath
Ray-o-vac
Reach
Realemon
Ritz
Sanka
Sara Lee
Saran Wrap
Simoniz
Special Dinners
Spic and Span
Stokely
Stouffer's
Stove Top
Stridex
Sunshine
Swift's
Tang
Tareyton
Taster's Choice

Teri	Unicap	Wesson
Tetley	Union Carbide	White Cloud
Top Choice	Van de Kamp's	Wisk
Trac II	Viva	Wondra
Tuna Helper	Vlasic	Wyler's
Ultra Ban	Waldorf	Yuban
Uncle Ben's	Waterpik	Zest
Underwood	Weight Watchers	Ziploc
	Welch's	

Selected Manufacturers' Addresses

Over the years, I have noticed an increased responsiveness by companies to consumer input and have provided below the addresses of some of the most popular companies that participate in refunds. These addresses are helpful if: (1) you don't receive a refund; (2) you particularly enjoy a product; (3) you have a problem with a product; or (4) you have a question about a product's use. Most companies are so happy to receive consumer letters that they respond with a thank you and a show of appreciation in the form of a sample or coupon.

In the event you are unsure of the company's name, check the label. In most cases you will find not only an address but also a toll-free number that can be used to reach the company. Good luck and happy refunding.

AIRWICK INDUSTRIES
1655 Valley Road
Wayne, NJ 07470
(201) 633-6700

Airwick products, Carpet Fresh, Chore Boy, Stick Ups

ALBERTO-CULVER CO.
2525 Armitage Avenue
Melrose Park, IL 60160
(708) 450-3000

Alberto VO5, Baker's Joy, New Dawn, Static Guard, Sugar Twin

AMERICAN HOME FOODS
685 Third Avenue
New York, NY 10017
(212) 878-6300

Chef Boy-Ar-Dee products, Crunch 'n Munch, Dennison's specialty foods, Gulden's mustard

ARMOUR SWIFT-ECKRICH
2001 Butterfield Road
Downers Grove, IL 60515
(708) 523-1000

Armour meats, Brown & Serve, Butterball, Eckrich, Peter Pan,

Sizzlean, Soup Starter, Swift

BEATRICE COS. INC.
2 North LaSalle Street
Chicago, IL 60602
(312) 558-4000

Swiss Miss

**BEECH-NUT NUTRITION
    CORP.**
Checkerboard Square
St. Louis, MO 63164
(314) 982-1679

Beech-Nut baby food

BEST FOODS BAKING GROUP
100 Passaic Avenue
Fairfield, NJ 07004
(201) 808-3000

Arnold breads, Brownberry

BORDEN INC.
180 East Broad Street
Columbus, OH 43215
(614) 225-4511

Borden products, Campfire marsh-
mallows, Cremora, Kava, Lite-
Line, None Such mincemeat

BOYLE-MIDWAY
685 Third Avenue
New York, NY 10017
(212) 986-1000

Aerowax, Black Flag, Easy-Off,
Easy-On, Old English, Sani-Flush,
Wizard, Woolite

BRISTOL-MYERS SQUIBB CO.
345 Park Avenue
New York, NY 10154
(212) 546-4000

Ban, Bufferin, Comtrex, Conges-
prin, Datril, Excedrin, No Doz,

Squibb, Theragran, Tickle

BUITONI FOODS CORP.
800 North Brand Boulevard
Glendale, CA 91203
(818) 549-6000

Buitoni products

C & C COLA CO. INC.
535 Dowd Avenue
Elizabeth, NJ 07201
(908) 289-4600

C & C soft drinks

CAMPBELL SOUP CO.
Campbell Place
Camden, NJ 08103-1799
(609) 342-4800

Campbell's, Franco-American,
Pepperidge Farm, Swanson

CHESEBROUGH-POND'S INC.
33 Benedict Place
Greenwich, CT 06830
(203) 661-2000 (800) 243-5300

Cutex, Pond's, Q-Tips, Vaseline
products

CLAIROL INC.
345 Park Avenue
New York, NY 10154
(212) 546-2775 (800) 223-5800

Born Beautiful, Clairesse, Final
Net, Frost & Tip, Happiness,
Herbal Essence, Loving Care, Miss
Clairol, Nice 'n Easy, Quiet Touch

CLOROX CO.
1221 Broadway
Oakland, CA 94612-1888
(510) 271-7000

Clorox, Formula 409, Liquid
Plumr, Litter Green, Pine-Sol, Soft

Scrub, Twice as Fresh

THE COCA-COLA CO.
Drawer 1734
Atlanta, GA 30301
(404) 676-2121

Bright & Early, Coca-Cola, Hi-C,
Minute Maid, Snow Crop

COLGATE-PALMOLIVE CO.
300 Park Avenue
New York, NY 10022
(212) 310-2000 (800) 221-4607

Ajax, Cashmere Bouquet, Cold
Power, Curad, Curity,
Dermassage, Dynamo, Fab, Fresh
Start, Handi Wipes, Irish Spring,
Mersene, Palmolive, Rapid Shave,
Wash 'n Dri

CONTINENTAL BAKING CO.
Checkerboard Square
St. Louis, MO 63164-0001
(314) 982-4700

County Fair, Ding Dongs, Fresh
& Natural, Fresh Horizons, Ho
Ho's, Home Pride, Hostess, Sno
Balls, Sunrise, Wonder

CPC INTERNATIONAL INC.
Box 8000
Englewood Cliffs, NJ 07632
(201) 894-4000

Golden Griddle syrup,
Hellmann's, Karo syrup, Knorr,
Mazola, Niagara starches, Nucoa
margarine, Rit dyes, Skippy,
Thomas' English muffins

THE CREAMETTE CO.
428 North First Street
Minneapolis, MN 55401
(612) 333-4281

Creamettes

DEL MONTE CORP.
Box 193575
San Francisco, CA 94119
(415) 442-4000
Del Monte food products, Milk-
mate, Ortega food products

DOLE FOODS CO.
31355 Oak Crest Drive
West Lake Village, CA 91361
(818) 879-6600

Dole fruit and vegetable products

DOWBRANDS
(Household Products Division)
Box 68511
Indianapolis, IN 46268
(317) 873-7000 (800) 428-4795

Dow cleaners, Handi-Wrap, Nova-
histine, Saran Wrap, Ziploc bags

THE DRACKETT CO.
201 East Fourth Street
Cincinnati, OH 45202
(513) 632-1800

Behold, Drano, Endust, Mr.
Muscle, O-Cedar, Renuzit,
Twinkle polish, Vanish, Windex

DURKEE FRENCH FOODS
1655 Valley Road
Wayne, NJ 07470
(201) 633-6800

Durkee's products

ENTENMANN'S
1724 Fifth Avenue
Bay Shore, NY 11706
(516) 273-6000 (800) 832-1440

Entenmann's baked goods

FISONS CORP.
755 Jefferson Road
Rochester, NY 14623
(716) 475-9000 (800) 235-5535

Allerest, Caldecort, Sinarest

FRITO-LAY INC.
Box 660634
Dallas, TX 75266-0634
(214) 351-7000 (800) 352-4477

Cheetos, Doritos, Funyuns,
Grandma's cookies, Munchos,
Rold Gold pretzels, Ruffles,
Tostitos

GENERAL FOODS USA
250 North Street
White Plains, NY 10625
(914) 335-2500 (800) 431-1003

Birds Eye, Brim, Calumet, Cool
Whip, Dream Whip, D-zerta,
Gravy Train, Jell-O, Kool-Aid,
Log Cabin, Minute Rice,
Northridge, Oroweat, Post,
Postum, Sanka, Shake 'n Bake,
Stove Top, Tang

GENERAL MILLS INC.
Box 1113
Minneapolis, MN 55440
(612) 540-2311

Betty Crocker, Bisquick, Cheerios,
Gold Medal flour, Kix, Lucky
Charms, Nature Valley, Total,
Tuna Helper, Wheaties

GERBER PRODUCTS CO.
445 State Street
Fremont, MI 49413
(616) 928-2000

Gerber baby products and foods

THE GILLETTE CO.
Prudential Tower Building
Boston, MA 02199
(617) 421-7000

Adorn, Atra, Dry Idea, Flair,
Good News, Mink Difference,
Right Guard, Toni hair products,
Trac II, White Rain, Widget

GREEN GIANT CO.
Pillsbury Center,
200 South Sixth Street
Minneapolis, MN 55402
(612) 330-4966 (800) 767-4466

Dawn Fresh, Green Giant

GREYHOUND-DIAL CORP.
Dial Tower, Dial Corp. Center
Phoenix, AZ 85077
(602) 207-2800

Appian Way, Borateem, Boraxo,
Breck, Bruce floor-care products,
Dial, Parsons' ammonia, Tone

H. J. HEINZ CO.
Box 57
Pittsburgh, PA 15230-0057
(412) 456-6128

Alba, Heinz

HERSHEY CHOCOLATE USA
19 East Chocolate Avenue
Hershey, PA 17033
(717) 534-4200 (800) 233-2145

Hershey's chocolate, Kit Kat

H. P. HOOD & SONS INC.
500 Rutherford Avenue
Boston, MA 02129
(617) 242-0600

Hood dairy products

GEO. A. HORMEL & CO.
501 Sixteenth Avenue Northeast
Austin, MN 55912
(507) 437-5611

Dinty Moore, Hormel, Mary
Kitchen

HUNT-WESSON INC.
1645 West Valencia Drive
Fullerton, CA 92633
(714) 680-1000

Hunt's, Manwich, Prima Salsa,
Orville Redenbacher's, Sunlite,
Wesson

THE ANDREW JERGENS CO.
2535 Spring Grove, Box 145444
Cincinnati, OH 45214
(513) 632-7744 (800) 222-3553

Gentle Touch, Jergens, Nature
Scents, Woodbury

JOHNSON & JOHNSON
501 George Street
New Brunswick, NJ 08903
(201) 524-0400 (800) 526-2433

Act, Band-Aids, Carefree, Modess,
O.B., Reach toothbrushes, Shower
to Shower, Stayfree, Sure &
Natural

KEEBLER CO.
1 Hollow Tree Lane
Elmhurst, IL 60126
(708) 833-2900

Keebler, Town House

THE KELLOGG CO.
1 Kellogg Square, Box 3599
Battle Creek, MI 49016-3599
(616) 961-2000

Kellogg's cereals, Pop-tarts

KIMBERLY-CLARK CORP.
401 North Lake Street
Neenah, WI 54956
(414) 721-2000

Anyday, Boutique, Casuals,
Delsey, Fems, Hi-Dri, Huggies,
Kleenex, Kleenguard spray, Kotex,
Lightdays, New Freedom, Teri
towels, Security, Vogue

KRAFT USA
Kraft Court
Glenview, IL 60025
(708) 998-2922 (800) 323-0768

Breakstone's, Breyers, Catalina,
Chiffon, Kraft Macaroni &
Cheese, Light n' Lively, Miracle
Whip, Parkay, Philadelphia,
Sealtest, Seven Seas, Velveeta

LAND O'LAKES INC.
Box 116
Minneapolis, MN 55440-0116
(612) 481-2222

Land O'Lakes dairy products

L'EGGS PRODUCTS INC.
Box 2495
Winston-Salem, NC 27102
(919) 768-9540

Sheer Elegance, Sheer Energy

LENDER'S BAGEL BAKERY
450 Island Lane
West Haven, CT 06516
(203) 934-9231

Lender's frozen bagels

LEVER BROS. CO. INC.
390 Park Avenue
New York, NY 10022
(212) 688-6000 (800) 223-0392

Aim, All, Breeze, Caress soap,
Close-Up, Dove, Drive, DX
toothbrushes, Final Touch,
Imperial margarine, Lifebuoy,
Lux, Mrs. Butterworth,
Pepsodent, Promise, Rinso, Shield,
Signal, Snuggle, Wisk

THOMAS J. LIPTON INC.
800 Sylvan Avenue
Englewood Cliffs, NJ 07632
(201) 567-8000

Knox gelatine, Lemon Tree,
Lipton soups, Lipton Tea products, Sunkist snack foods, Wishbone, Wyler's drinks

M & M/MARS INC.
6885 Elm Street
McLean, VA 22101
(703) 821-4900

M & M's, Marathon, Mars, Milky
Way, Starburst Chews, Summit,
Three Musketeers, Twix

McCORMICK & CO. INC.
18 Loveton Circle, Box 6000
Sparks, MD 21152-6000
(410) 527-6000 (800) 331-3833

Cake-Mate, McCormick/Schilling,
Tio Sancho seasoning mixes

McNEIL CONSUMER
   PRODUCTS CO.
7050 Camp Hill Road
Fort Washington, PA 19034
(215) 233-7000 (800) 225-8263

CoTylenol, Sine-Aid, Tylenol

MARCAL PAPER MILLS INC.
1 Market Street
Elmwood Park, NJ 07407
(201) 796-4000 (800) 631-8451

Marcal paper products

MILES INC.
1127 Murttle Street
Elkhart, IN 46514
(219) 264-8716

Alka-Seltzer, Bactine, Chocks,
Flintstones, One-A-Day, S.O.S.
pads, Tuffy

MOBIL CHEMICAL CO.
(Consumer Products Division)
1159 Pittsford Victor Road
Pittsford, NY 14534
(716) 248-5700

JOHN MORRELL & CO.
250 East Fifth Street
Cincinnati, OH 45202
(513) 852-3500

Hunter meats, John Morrell
meats, Rodeo meat

MORTON INTERNATIONAL
   INC.
(Morton Salt Division)
100 North Riverside Plaza
Chicago, IL 60606
(312) 807-2000

Morton salt

MRS. PAUL'S KITCHENS
5501 Tabor Road
Philadelphia, PA 19120
(215) 535-1151

Mrs. Paul's products

NABISCO BRANDS INC.
100 DeForest
East Hanover, NJ 07936
(201) 503-2000 (800) 223-1049

A-1 sauce, Blue Bonnet, Chips
Ahoy, Cream of Wheat, Curtiss

candy, Egg Beaters, Fig Newtons, Grey Poupon mustard, Lorna Doone, Milk-Bone, Mister Salty pretzels, Nabisco, Oreo, Premium, Regina wine vinegars, Ritz, Royal gelatin, Shredded Wheat, Steak Supreme sauce

NESTLÉ BEVERAGE CO.
345 Spear Street
San Francisco, CA 94105
(415) 546-4600 (800) 637-8531

Nescafé, Nestea, Quik, Sunrise, Tasters Choice

NESTLÉ USA
800 North Brand Boulevard
Glendale, CA 91203
(818) 549-6000

Bright Eyes, Chef's Blend, Contadina, Friskies, Libby, Nestlé chocolate, Slender

NOXELL CORP.
11050 York Road
Hunt Valley, MD 21030
(410) 785-7300 (800) 638-6204

Cover Girl, Moisturewear, Noxzema

ORE-IDA FOODS INC.
Box 10
Boise, ID 83707
(208) 383-6100

La Pizzeria, Ore-Ida

OSCAR MAYER FOODS CORP.
910 Mayer Avenue
Madison, WI 53704-4287
(608) 241-3311

Oscar Mayer meat products

PEPSI-COLA CO.
1 Pepsi Way
Somers, NY 10589
(914) 767-6000 (800) 237-3774

Diet Pepsi, Mountain Dew, Pepsi-Cola, Pepsi Free, Pepsi Light, Slice, Teem

PET INC.
Box 393
St. Louis, MO 63166
(314) 622-7700 (800) 325-7130

Ac'cent, Downyflakes, Van de Kamp's food products

THE PILLSBURY CO.
Pillsbury Center,
200 South Sixth Street
Minneapolis, MN 55402-1464
(612) 330-4966 (800) 767-4466

Farina, Hungry Jack, Pillsbury food products

PLAYTEX MARKETING CORP.
708 Third Avenue
New York, NY 10017
(212) 953-4304

Playtex products

PLUMROSE INC.
Box 160
Elkhart, IN 46515
(219) 295-8190

PROCTER & GAMBLE CO.
Box 599
Cincinnati, OH 45201
(513) 983-1100 (800) 543-7270

Biz, Bold 3, Bonus, Bounce, Bounty, Camay, Cascade, Charmin, Cheer, Coast, Comet, Crest, Crisco, Dash, Dawn, Downy, Dreft, Duncan Hines, Duz, Fluffo, Gain,

Gleem, Head & Shoulders, High Point, Ivory, Ivory Snow, Jif, Joy, Kirk, Lava, Lestoil, Lilt, Luvs, Mr. Clean, Old Spice, Oxydol, Pampers, Pert, Prell, Pringle's, Puffs, Puritan, Safeguard, Salvo, Scope, Secret, Spic and Span, Sure, Thrill, Tide, Top Job, White Cloud, Wondra, Zest

THE QUAKER OATS CO.
Box 9003-049001
Chicago, IL 60604-9001
(312) 222-7111

Aunt Jemima, Celeste, Flako, Gaines pet products, Ken-L-Ration, Life, Puss 'n Boots, Quaker food products, Top Choice

RALSTON PURINA CO.
Checkerboard Square
St. Louis, MO 63164
(314) 982-1000 (800) 345-5678

Bonz, Butcher's Blend, Chex, Cookie Crisp, Country Stand, Good Mews, Happy Cat, High Protein, Mainstay, Ocean Blend, Purina, Tender Vittles, Whisker Lickins

RAYOVAC CORP.
601 Rayovac Drive
Madison, WI 53711
(800) 223-8533

Rayovac batteries and flashlights

REVLON INC.
625 Madison Avenue
New York, NY 10022
(212) 527-4000

Charlie, Eterna 27, European Collagen Complex, Mitchum, Moon Drops, Natural Wonder, Revlon

RICHARDSON-VICKS USA
1 Far Mill Crossing
Shelton, CT 06484
(203) 925-6000

Clearasil, Complete denture cleanser, Day-care, Fasteeth, Fixadent, Formula 44, Kleenite, Nyquil, Oil of Olay, Sinex, Topex, Vicks

RIVIANA FOODS INC.
Box 2636
Houston, TX 77252
(713) 529-3251

Carolina, River, Success, Water Maid rices

RJR FOODS INC.
1301 Avenue of the Americas
New York, NY 10019
(212) 258-5600

Chun King, College Inn, Hawaiian Punch, My-T-Fine desserts, Vermont Maid

SARA LEE CORP.
3 First National Plaza Building
70 West Madison Street
Chicago, IL 60602
(312) 726-2600

Kahn ham steaks, Sara Lee frozen foods

SCOTT PAPER CO.
Scott Plaza
Philadelphia, PA 19113
(215) 522-5000

Baby Fresh, Cottonelle, Cut-Rite wax paper, Job Squad, Scott, Scotties, Soft-Weve, Viva, Waldorf

SMITHKLINE BEECHAM
(Consumer Products Division)
100 Beecham Drive
Pittsburgh, PA 15205
(412) 928-1000

Aqua-fresh, Aqua Velva, Brylcreem,
Calgon, Cling Free, Deep Down,
Esoterica, Femiron, Fruit-fresh,
Geritol, Massengill, Nature's
Remedy, Rose Milk, Serutan,
Somminex, Sucrets, Tums, Vivarin

THE J. M. SMUCKER CO.
Strawberry Lane
Orrville, OH 44667
(216) 682-0015

Smucker's jellies

STARKIST FOODS INC.
180 East Ocean Boulevard
Long Beach, CA 90802
(213) 590-7900

Star-Kist tuna

STERLING WINTHROP
90 Park Avenue
New York, NY 10016
(212) 907-2000

Bayer, Diaperene, Midol, Phillips'
Milk of Magnesia, Vanquish

STOUFFER FOODS CORP.
30003 Bainbridge Road
Solon, OH 44139
(216) 248-3600
(800) 225-1180

Stouffer's foods

TETLEY INC.
100 Commerce Drive
Shelton, CT 06484
(203) 929-9200

Brown Gold, Martinson, Savarin,
Tetley Tea

TREESWEET PRODUCTS CO.
16825 Northchase Street,
Suite 1600,
Houston, TX 77060
(713) 876-3759

Fruit juices

TREE TOP INC.
Box 248
Selah, WA 98942
(509) 697-7251

Fruit juices

TROPICANA PRODUCTS INC.
Box 338
Bradenton, FL 34206
(813) 747-4461 (800) 237-9611

Fruit juices
TYSON FOODS INC.
Box 2020,
Springdale, AR 72765
(501) 756-4000

Weaver poultry products
UNCLE BEN'S INC.
Box 1752,
5721 Harvey Wilson Drive,
Houston, TX 77251
(713) 674-9484

Uncle Ben's rice products
VAN DEN BERGH FOODS CO.
21 Third Street Northwest
Madelia, MN 56062
(507) 642-3323

Mrs. Filbert's margarine, Shedd's

VLASIC FOODS INC.
26777 Halstead Road, #100
Farmington Hills, MI 48331-3541
(313) 473-2305

Open Pit, Vlasic foods

WARNER-LAMBERT CO.
201 Tabor Road
Morris Plains, NJ 07950
(201) 540-2000 (800) 223-0182

Bromo Seltzer, Efferdent,
Freshen-Up, Listerine, Personal
Touch, Schick Razors, Ultrex

WEATHERLY CONSUMER
   PRODUCTS INC.
Box 1750, Lexington, KY 40593
(606) 263-3633

WEIGHT WATCHERS
   INTERNATIONAL INC.
519 North Broadway
Jericho, NY 11753
(516) 939-0400 (800) 333-3000

Weight Watchers products

WELCH FOODS INC.
100 Main Street
Concord, MA 01742
(508) 371-1000

Welch's drinks

WILSON FOODS CORP.
2601 Northwest Expressway,
Suite 1000 W.
Oklahoma City, OK 73112
(405) 879-5500

Certified, Corn King, and Wilson
meat products

UPCs of Selected Products

Most UPCs contain a ten-digit number below the piano bar symbol, while others have only a six-digit number. Where there is a ten-digit number, the first four or five digits indicate the manufacturer of the product, the next two or three identify the product, and the final digits identify the product size and variety. For six-digit codes, the first two digits identify the manufacturer, the next two identify the product, and the final two identify product size and variety.

Below is a list of some common product UPCs. This list does not contain product sizes and varieties; such an exhaustive listing would require its own book. Many common products are not listed, again partly out of space considerations but also because many of those unlisted are products that state the product name directly above the UPC.

The First Six to Eight Digits of Some Common Product Ten-Digit UPCs

The manufacturer prefix is listed first, followed by individual product codes, which appear immediately after the prefix in the UPC, of the manufacturer. The list contains the shortest possible codes that will identify a product line.

00450: Tylenol (McNeil
    Laboratories)
01490: Pepto-Bismol (Procter &
    Gamble)
0573: Whitehall Laboratories
    015: Advil

020: Anacin
29: Primatene
1111: Lever Bros.
    132: Lever 2000
    140: Dove Dishwashing
        Detergent

143 & 147: Sun Light
148: Surf
156: Snuggle
158: Final Touch
161: Dove soap
165: Sunlight
171: Shield
173: Caress
187: Wisk
189: All
374 & 379: Close-Up
11115: Van den Bergh
83: Promise
87: Imperial
12547: Warner-Lambert
639: Efferdent
701: Listerine
12587: Glad products (First Brands)
12483: Bayer
165400: Miles, Inc.
04: Alka-Seltzer
13000: Heinz
008: Vinegar
45: Beans
137002: Hefty Products (Mobil Chemical Co.)
15000: Gerber
00: Cereals
012: Foods
022: Foods and juices
026: Foods
17800: Ralston Purina
404,5: Puppy Chow
419: Dog Chow
528: Hi-Pro
18000: Pillsbury
204, 213, 457: Flours
19810: Bristol-Myers Squibb
001: Excedrin
005: Bufferin

076: Nuprin
20000: Pillsbury
10, 12: Green Giant
21000: Kraft-General Foods
25: Baker's Chocolate
60-62: Cheeses
640: Mayonnaise
644: Dressings
645: Miracle Whip
65: Parkay
72: Velveeta
224000 & 224001: VO5 (Alberto-Culver)
22700: Noxzema (Procter & Gamble)
23900: Procter & Gamble
00: Nyquil
01: Chloraseptic
24200: Purex
25700: Dow Products
001: Saran Wrap
002: Handi-Wrap
003: Ziploc
011: Saran Wrap
25000: Coca-Cola
004: 5 Alive
026: Minute Maid
27000: Hunt-Wesson
382: Ketchup
432: Old Country Sauce
441: Manwich
485-89: Orville Redenbacher
612: Wesson Oil
27400: Shedd's (Van den Bergh)
28000: Nestlé
080: Raisinets
160: Crunch
214,5: Toll House Morsels

241, 3: Quik
330, 39, 44: Nestea
346, 54: Ice Teaser
29800: Royal (Nabisco)
29100: Breck
30000: Ken-L Ration
34000: Hershey's
    040: Cadbury's
    076: Kit Kat
    132: Kisses
    14: Chocolate chips
    17: Chocolate bars
    218: Miniatures
    405: Reese's
35000: Colgate Palmolive
    143: Irish Spring
    405: Dynamo
    421: Fab
    426, 66, 73, 75:
      Palmolive Dish
      Detergent
    50, 1, 6, 7, 9:
      Colgate toothpaste
36000: Kimberly-Clark
    261, 77, 85, 96: Kleenex
    52: Huggies
36200: Ragu (Van den Bergh)
36632: Dannon
37000: Procter & Gamble
    004: Crisco or Jif
    005: Comet
    0073: Top Job
    0078, 342: Spic and
      Span
    053: Ajax
    303, 706: Ivory soap
    31: Zest
    32: Safeguard
    331: Mr. Clean

339: Lestoil
35: Downy
41, 42: Duncan Hines
60: Charmin
61: White Cloud
62: Puffs
64: Luvs
65: Pampers
63: Bounty
67: Summit
702: Prell
703: Head & Shoulders
708: Pert
713,155: Secret
717: Sure
904: Dreft
914: Era
918, 922, 927: Tide
932, 951, 970: Cheer
939: Joy
940, 975: Dawn
950: Cascade
960: Solo
39800: Everready
    01-3: Energizer
40000: M&M Mars
    016, 068: Milky Way
    152, 351, 051, 057:
      M&M
    168: Dove
41000: Lipton
    01: Soup mixes
    022: Rice and noodle
      mixes
41196: Progresso (Pet)
41333: Duracell
41771: Kodak
    16, 53, 82: Batteries
42000: James River

02: Northern Napkins
35: Vanity Fair
43000: Kraft
103: Tang
200, 01, 04, 06: Jell-O
220-2: Minute Rice
704, 47: Maxwell
House
940, 53, 55: Kool-Aid
950: Crystal Light
951, 2: Country Time
966, 7, 9: Jell-O
43800: Buitoni (Nestlé)
44600: Clorox Co.
0002: Soft Scrub
006: Formula 409
46500: S. C. Johnson
004: Pledge
019: Agree
02: Halsa
48001: Best Foods
26: Hellman's
05: Mazola
50000: Nestlé
04, 34: Contadina
51000: Campbell
012, 027, 050: Prego
064, 52: Spaghetti-o's
08, 09: Swanson
40: Healthy Choice
53100: Aqua Fresh
53875: Hershey's Puddings
54000: Scott
18:Towels
19: Viva
46: Scott-tissue
49: Cottonelle
58: Napkins
7: Sofkins

85: Scotties
54600: Dow Brands
001: Yes
003: Fantastik
54800: Uncle Ben's
04: Converted Rice
201: Country Inn
74182: Chesebrough-Ponds
052: Rave
262: Softsoap
267: Sesame Street soap
products
76100: PermaSoft (Dow Brands)
79400: Helene Curtis
75: Suave
8137: Johnson & Johnson

The First Three to Five Digits of Some Six-Digit UPCs

13: Heinz
12: Ketchup
45: Baked Beans
29: Mueller's (Best Foods)
37: Procter & Gamble
07, 09: Pert
28-39: Crest
41: Lipton
28: Tea bags
32: Soup mixes
41: Recipe Mix
55, 62-68: Wishbone
75, 84, 86: Iced tea mixes

434: Birds Eye
453: Peter Pan (Hunt-Wesson)
522-525: Beech Nut baby foods
54: Nabisco
48: Regina

State Abbreviations

Alabama	AL	Missouri	MO
Alaska	AK	Montana	MT
Arizona	AZ	Nebraska	NE
Arkansas	AR	Nevada	NV
California	CA	New Hampshire	NH
Colorado	CO	New Jersey	NJ
Connecticut	CT	New Mexico	NM
Delaware	DE	New York	NY
District of Columbia	DC	North Carolina	NC
Florida	FL	North Dakota	ND
Georgia	GA	Ohio	OH
Hawaii	HI	Oklahoma	OK
Idaho	ID	Oregon	OR
Illinois	IL	Pennsylvania	PA
Indiana	IN	Rhode Island	RI
Iowa	IA	South Carolina	SC
Kansas	KS	South Dakota	SD
Kentucky	KY	Tennessee	TN
Louisiana	LA	Texas	TX
Maine	ME	Utah	UT
Maryland	MD	Vermont	VT
Massachusetts	MA	Washington	WA
Michigan	MI	West Virginia	WV
Minnesota	MN	Wisconsin	WI
Mississippi	MS	Wyoming	WY

Clearinghouse Addresses

Douglas, AZ	85655
Phoenix, AZ	85072
Sierra Vista, AZ	85670
Clinton, IA	52736
Kankakee, IL	60902
Mt. Prospect, IL	60056
Baltimore, MD	21268
Ridgely, MD	21681
Bloomington, MN	55438
Grand Rapids, MN	55745
Minneapolis, MN	55440
Monticello, MN	55563, 55565
Norwood, MN	55583
Young America, MN	55551, 55573
Jefferson City, MO	65102
Dallas, TX	75380
El Paso, TX	88540, 88541, 88542, 88543, 88547

— REFUNDER'S LOG —

	COMPANY	OFFER NAME	REFUND ADDRESS	FORM USED	QUALIFIERS NEEDED	QUALIFIERS ON HAND	DATE SENT	DATE RECEIVED	AMOUNT	COMMENTS
1										
2										
3										
4										
5										
6										
7										
8										
9										
10										
11										
12										
13										
14										
15										